# MID-ATLANTIC LIGHTHOUSES

# BY BRUCE ROBERTS *and* RAY JONES

Southern Lighthouses
*Chesapeake Bay to the Gulf of Mexico*

Eastern Great Lakes Lighthouses
*Ontario, Erie, and Huron*

Western Great Lakes Lighthouses
*Michigan and Superior*

Western Lighthouses
*Olympic Peninsula to San Diego*

New England Lighthouses
*Bay of Fundy to Long Island Sound*

Mid-Atlantic Lighthouses
*Hudson River to Chesapeake Bay*

# *Mid-Atlantic*

# LIGHTHOUSES

## HUDSON RIVER *to* CHESAPEAKE BAY

PHOTOGRAPHS *by* BRUCE ROBERTS
TEXT *by* RAY JONES

The
Globe
Pequot
Press

Guilford, Connecticut

*The Old Point Comfort Lighthouse flashes its warning to mariners just as it has done for nearly two centuries. Tinted window panes make the flash appear red to those seeing it from the seaward side. The heart of any lighthouse is, of course, its lighting apparatus—in this case, a handmade Fresnel lens, which concentrates the light into a powerful, narrow beam. Manufactured in Paris during the nineteenth century, the Fresnels came in a variety of sizes called "orders." These ranged from sixth-order (about seventeen inches high and a foot wide) to first-order (as much as ten feet high and six feet wide). The Old Point Comfort Fresnel is a modest, fourth-order lens.*

Copyright © 1989, 1990, 1994, 1995, 1996 by Bruce Roberts and Ray Jones

All photographs, unless otherwise credited, are by Bruce Roberts.

Book design by Nancy Freeborn

**Library of Congress Cataloging-in-Publication Data**
Roberts, Bruce.
    Mid-Atlantic lighthouses : Hudson River to Chesapeake Bay /
photographs by Bruce Roberts : text by Ray Jones. — 2nd ed.
       p.  cm. — (Lighthouses series)

    Includes bibliographical references  (p. 81) and index.
    ISBN 1-56440-984-8
    1. Lighthouses—Mid-Atlantic.  I. Jones, Ray.  II. Title.
III. Series : Lighthouse series (Old Saybrook, Conn.)
VK1024.N38R625  1996
387.1'55'0974—dc20                   96-18770
                                   CIP

*Front-cover photograph: Thomas Point Lighthouse, Chesapeake Bay, Maryland*
*Front-cover photograph: Concord Point Lighthouse, Havre de Grace, Maryland*

Printed in Quebec, Canada
First Edition / Sixth Printing

To the men and women of the old United States Lighthouse Service.
They transformed the darkness along the shore into points of light
that gave America the best-lighted coastline in the world.

—*Bruce Roberts*


To the children of America's lighthouse keepers.

—*Ray Jones*

*Its light shining above the horizon like a setting sun, the Cape May Lighthouse towers regally above the southern New Jersey shore. This extraordinary, 600,000-candlepower beacon is one of the most important navigational lights on the U.S. east coast.*

# ACKNOWLEDGMENTS

We gratefully acknowledge the assistance of the following people in the making of this book: U.S. Coast Guard Historian Dr. Robert Browning; photographer Bill Kaufhold; photographer Mark Riddick; photographer Frank Parks; photographers Bob and Sandra Shanklin; Tom Laverty of the Navesink Lighthouse in New Jersey; Candace Clifford of the Maritime Initiative in Washington, D.C.; Jack Barbara of Edison for his assistance with locations of lighthouses in New Jersey; Zoe Madans of New Jersey for generous contacts concerning mid-Atlantic lighthouses; the Mariners Museum Library of Newport News, the Chesapeake Bay Maritime Museum at Saint Michaels, Maryland, and the Calvert Marine Museum in Solomons, Maryland, all of which have excellent historical materials that they made available to us.

# CONTENTS

*The Fenwick Island Lighthouse marks a dark stretch of coast near the Maryland–Delaware border. The famed Mason-Dixon Line runs through the station property.*

# INTRODUCTION

The ancient Greeks were a seafaring people, so it should come as no surprise that they included a lighthouse among their Seven Wonders of the World. Along with the Pyramids of Egypt, the Hanging Gardens of Babylon, the Colossus of Rhodes, and the other wonders, they ranked Pharos, history's first great lighthouse, among the most important and spectacular manmade structures of any age. Rising 450 feet into the blue Mediterranean skies, Pharos was also the tallest lighthouse of all time—and, as twelve centuries of nearly continuous operation would prove, the light with the longest service record.

Built about 280 B.C. on an island in the bustling harbor of the Greco-Egyptian city Alexandria, Pharos guided ships to the world's busiest seaport. The light, produced by a fire blazing on the tower's roof, could be seen from nearly thirty miles at sea. Ancient mariners needed the Pharos light because Alexandria stood on the flat Nile Delta, and there were no mountains or other natural features to help them locate the city from the sea.

Peoples had long made a practice of banking fires on hills and mountainsides to bring their sailors home from the sea. With Pharos, its artificial mountain, Alexandria pulled in seamen from the entire known world. The sight of the Pharos light burning far up near the dome of the sky must have filled the breasts of countless sea captains with awe. In time the delta city became the busiest and most prosperous port on Earth, and it remained so for nearly a thousand years.

Trading ships from Greece, Carthage, and Rome flocked to the city's wharves to load up with the grain grown in wondrous abundance along the banks of the Nile. It was for possession of Alexandria and her grain markets that Octavius fought and defeated Antony and Cleopatra. Without Egypt's grain to feed the empire's teeming city masses, Rome's conquests would have been meaningless. And without Pharos, the lumbering Roman grain ships might never have found Alexandria. Thus, in a very real sense, the Roman Empire depended on a lighthouse.

Like Rome, the United States of America is a highly commercial nation, part industrial and part agrarian. As with Rome, the growth and prosperity of the United States has depended on safe navigation of waters leading to its busy port cities. As a result, lighthouses have been a major concern for Americans right from the nation's beginning. This book tells the story of the lighthouses that serve America's vital Mid-Atlantic coast from New York to Virginia. (See also our other informative and colorful lighthouses volumes: *New England Lighthouses, Southern Lighthouses, Western Lighthouses, Western Great Lakes Lighthouses,* and *Eastern Great Lakes Lighthouses.*)

## AMERICA'S OWN TINY PHAROS

America also has a proud old city named Alexandria, and it, too, is a port. Like the first Alexandria, the city in Virginia was once the heart of a rich agricultural region. Today it is a wealthy suburb, located down the Potomac River from the nation's capital.

Alexandria is a historic city. It was here that George Washington, who lived only a short carriage ride away in Mount Vernon, did most of his shopping and socializing. At his club in Alexandria, Washington

*Looking a bit like an old one-room schoolhouse, the Jones Point Lighthouse marks the way to Alexandria, Virginia, and Washington, D.C., for ships and boaters on the Potomac River. Built in 1855, this river light is the nation's oldest.* (© Mark Riddick/New Light Photography)

met with friends and advisers to plan the strategy that would carry him and the nation through the Revolutionary War.

After the war had established America's independence, Alexandria was among the cities proposed to become the nation's new capital. In fact, Alexandria was included within the original boundaries of the District of Columbia, but eventually its citizens chose to cast their lot with agrarian Virginia. At Alexandria's Jones Point, some five or six miles down the Potomac from the City of Washington, is a stone marking one of the corners of the old ten-square-mile federal district.

Also at Jones Point stands a small, rectangular building with whitewashed wooden walls, a pitched roof, and a raised porch. Probably no more than twenty feet high, its appearance suggests a nineteenth-century country schoolhouse. Except for the tiny lantern protruding from its roof, one might never guess that it had anything in common with the Pharos tower of ancient Egypt's Alexandria. But it does: It is a lighthouse.

Built in 1855, the Jones Point Lighthouse guided trading ships, tugs, and barges into Alexandria, Washington, and nearby Georgetown for more than seventy years. It can now claim distinction as the nation's oldest standing inland lighthouse. In counterpoint to its gargantuan Egyptian ancestor, it is also among the nation's and the world's smallest lighthouses.

Deactivated in 1926, the venerable little lighthouse was abandoned. Eventually it fell into a sad state of disrepair. It might have been torn down had it not been for the intervention of the Daughters of the American Revolution and other groups concerned with the preservation of historic structures.

The story of the Jones Point Lighthouse has a happy ending. It recently received a much-needed facelift, and today it has a new, active life—in 1995, after nearly seven decades of disuse, its lantern was relit. Pleasure craft and other vessels headed up the Potomac at night will now see a light burning on Jones Point, just as Roman sea captains once saw a fire burning over the Nile Delta.

## THE LIGHTHOUSE REVOLUTION

Lighthouses were among the flash points where trading ships and history collided to produce the nation we know today. In 1718 Alexander Spotswood, the governor of colonial Virginia, approached the British Board of Trade with a remarkable idea. Why not build a tower on Cape Henry, at the mouth of the Chesapeake, and place a light atop it to guide ships into the bay? Just such a tower had been built a couple of years earlier in Massachusetts, and as a result, Boston Harbor had become a magnet for sea trade almost overnight. Governor Spotswood was certain that a similar structure erected on one of the Virginia capes not only would make the Chesapeake Bay safer for shipping but also would greatly increase commerce in the region. Spotswood told the British that the benefits of the project seemed to him "so obvious that I have often wondered why so useful a work has not been undertaken long ere now."

The Board of Trade listened politely to the governor's proposal and then proceeded to ignore it. The British government had begun to grow suspicious and, perhaps, a touch envious of the swelling prosperity of its colonies in America. Parliament had no intention of spending good British sterling on a project likely to help the business-minded American colonists make still more money. So the British built no lighthouse on Cape Henry. More than half a century later, General Charles Cornwallis may have wished they had.

By the mid-1770s British subjects in the American colonies were fed up with their mother country. They hated paying taxes—even a penny a pound tax on tea—and the negligent attitude of British officials toward needed public projects, such as the building of lighthouses, made the colonists even more obstinate about opening their purses for the king. It seemed to them that His Majesty George III considered them a lot of country bumpkins. Feeling that they were being treated like second-class citizens, increasing numbers of Americans were reaching the conclusion that they must take their destinies into their own hands.

Caught up in the independent spirit sweeping the colonies, the people of Maryland and Virginia decided to pool their resources and build their own lighthouse on Cape Henry. In their view, if the project were left entirely to the British, the mouth of the Chesapeake would be dark forever. But work on the lighthouse had barely started when the alienation of Americans boiled over into open rebellion, and the effort had to be abandoned. Instead of constructing a lighthouse, the colonists now undertook to build a nation of their own.

The Revolutionary War was very hard on lighthouses. The British blew up North America's oldest lighthouse when they retreated from Boston in 1776. Another early light, the Cape Henlopen Lighthouse, which dated to 1765, was snuffed out by the British in 1777. It would not be repaired and back on active duty again until well after the end of the war.

Although the Treaty of Paris, granting Americans their independence from Britain, was not signed until 1783, most historians agree that the war ended in 1781 at Yorktown, Virginia. By August of that year, when General Cornwallis marched his redcoat army into Yorktown, the British had been fighting for

*The octagonal stone tower of the Old Cape Henry Lighthouse was built in 1792. A "newer" tower, completed in 1881, stands nearby.*

five long and wearying years to put down the American revolt.

Tired of the struggle, they had sent Cornwallis to America with orders to bring the war to a speedy conclusion. Tough and ruthless, Cornwallis had no scruples at all about burning people's homes and crops and driving off their livestock. He was sent to America to heap misery on the king's unruly subjects, and, in a series of destructive sweeps through the Carolinas and Virginia during the spring and summer of 1781, that is exactly what he did. Then, believing smugly that he had brought the revolutionaries to their knees, Cornwallis fell back to rest and resupply his troops at Yorktown, a small port located conveniently on the banks of the York River near the point where it flows into the Chesapeake.

Cornwallis had one important flaw as a commander: an arrogant disregard for the military skill of his opponents. He had little respect for the fighting abilities of the French, who had entered the war on the side of the Americans, and even less for George Washington and his ragtag Continental Army. So, even with his back to the York River and the Chesapeake beyond, Cornwallis felt perfectly safe at Yorktown. Indeed, he was so confident that he neglected to hurry his soldiers in their task of fortifying his new base of operations.

It must have astounded the British general to learn, as he did in mid-September, that Washington's army was closing in on Yorktown. Marching alongside the Virginia planter and his soldiers was a large body of French infantry as well as a second army under the Marquis de Lafayette. The startled Cornwallis realized that he would soon be dangerously outnumbered.

But the general remained calm. He knew that he had a resource near at hand that the Americans could not hope to match—the British Navy. He had every reason to believe that a fleet of friendly ships would soon appear and, with their massed cannons, send his enemies fleeing into the woods. Cornwallis felt sure that, at the very least, he could count on the Royal Navy to evacuate his troops.

Exactly as Cornwallis thought, help was on its way; a large British squadron of twenty-seven ships, commanded by Admiral Thomas Graves, was pushing south from New York under full sail. But the relief squadron never reached Yorktown. Just as Graves cut eastward toward the Chesapeake at the Virginia capes, he slammed into an unexpected obstacle: A powerful fleet of thirty-six French warships under Rear Admiral De Grasse blocked the way. Had there been a lighthouse on Cape Henry to show the way, Graves might have slipped past the French fleet in the night, entered the Chesapeake, and rescued the beleaguered Cornwallis. But with no lighthouse on the cape to guide his ships, Graves dared not attempt such a maneuver. He had no alternative but to attack. Cannons flashed and thundered for hour after hour. When the battle was over, three British fighting ships had been sunk and the rest were fleeing north in disorder.

Cornwallis's proud redcoats now found themselves tightly squeezed between Americans and French to their front and the York River at their back. The British crouched low in their trenches as cannonballs rained in from several directions. The artillery barrage became so fierce that Cornwallis had to move his headquarters into a cave under the bluffs along the Yorktown waterfront. To prevent French ships from sailing into the harbor and shelling him from the rear, Cornwallis created artificial shoals in the river by scuttling supply boats.

The British fought on for several weeks, but with no help coming from beyond the capes, the outcome of the siege was no longer in question. On October 20, 1781, their band playing a tune called "The World Turned Upside Down," the redcoats marched out from behind their fortifications and surrendered. The Americans had won the Revolutionary War and with it the right to collect their own taxes—and, if they wished, to build their own lighthouses.

What course might history have taken if the British had built a lighthouse on the Virginia Capes shortly after 1718, when the colonists first asked for it? Had the British been more solicitous of the colonists and paid closer attention to their needs, maybe there would never have been a revolution in the first place. Even if the split was inevitable, the Battle of Yorktown and the war itself might have turned out differently if there had been a lighthouse on Cape Henry to guide the British fleet to Cornwallis's rescue.

Roughly a dozen years after the Yorktown siege and less than ten years after the Treaty of Paris made the American independence official, the United States government built a lighthouse on Cape Henry. Completed in 1792, it stood very near the place where, a lifetime earlier, Governor Spotswood had envisioned a tower. Spotswood died in 1740, many years before the Revolution, independence, and construction of the Cape Henry Lighthouse. But, had he lived to see it, the sight of a light burning on the cape would surely have brought a knowing smile to his face.

*As is the case with many lighthouses now serving as museums, the Drum Point Light, in Solomons, Maryland, contains many artifacts from an earlier era.*

*The Tarrytown Lighthouse in New York stands with its feet in the Hudson River. Exposed to wind, high water, and winter ice, it is armored with heavy, steel plates. For obvious reasons, lighthouses of this type are sometimes called "spark plugs."* (© William Kaufhold)

# CHAPTER ONE

# Lights at
# THE GOLDEN DOOR
## NEW YORK

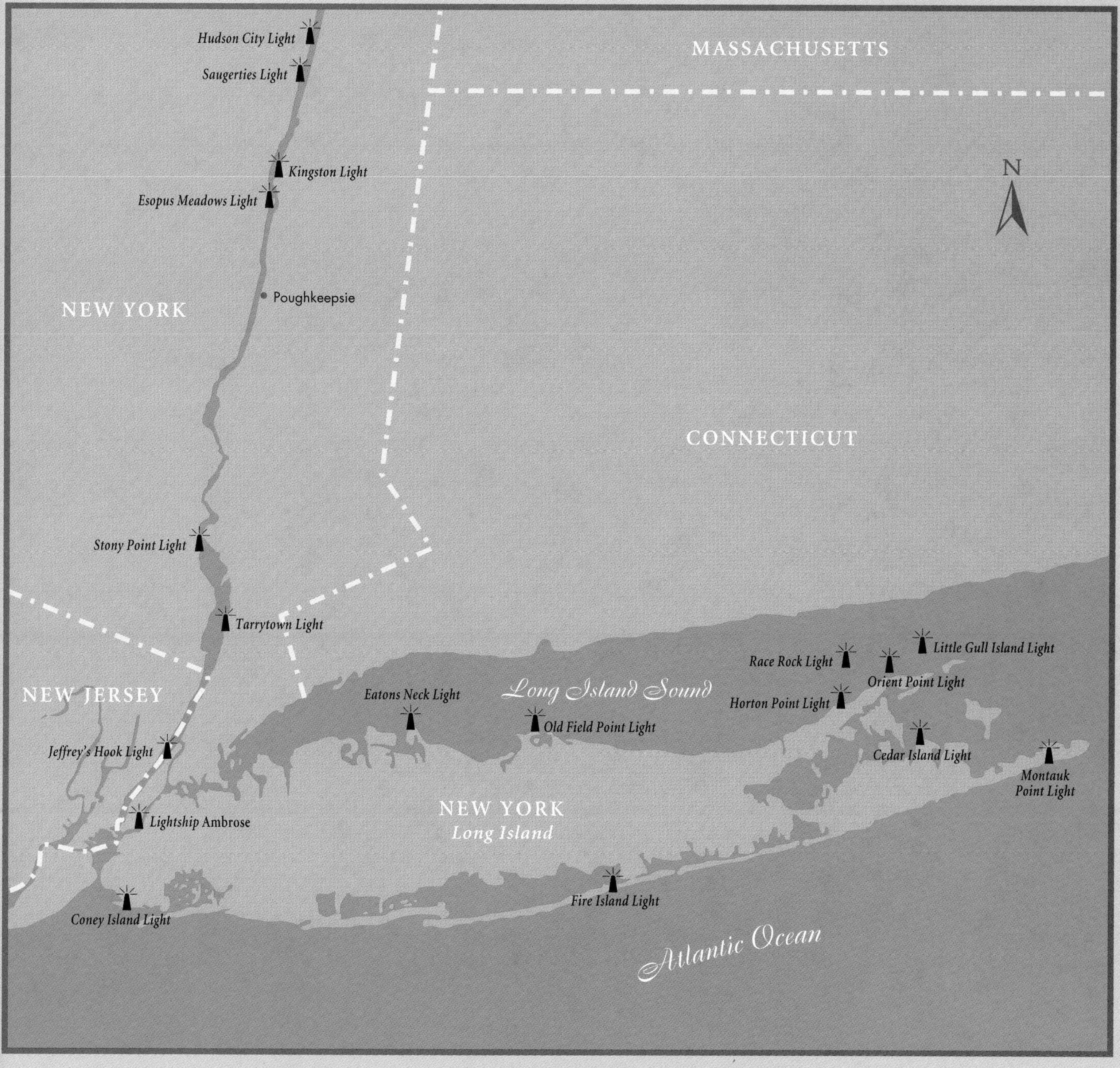

Hudson City Light

Saugerties Light

Kingston Light

Esopus Meadows Light

MASSACHUSETTS

N

Poughkeepsie

NEW YORK

CONNECTICUT

Stony Point Light

Tarrytown Light

Little Gull Island Light

Race Rock Light

Orient Point Light

NEW JERSEY

Eatons Neck Light

Long Island Sound

Horton Point Light

Old Field Point Light

Cedar Island Light

Montauk Point Light

Jeffrey's Hook Light

Lightship Ambrose

NEW YORK
Long Island

Coney Island Light

Fire Island Light

Atlantic Ocean

*America's oldest standing lighthouse, the Sandy Hook Light has pointed the way to New York City and the mouth of the Hudson since 1764. It has been in continuous operation—more than two-and-a-quarter centuries—for longer than any other American lighthouse.* (© William Kaufhold)

A farmer and a lifelong landlubber, George Washington rarely went to sea, but, like Governor Spotswood before him, he was a friend and enthusiastic promoter of lighthouses. In 1789, as president, Washington urged the very first U.S. Congress to pass legislation taking federal control of all coastal lighthouses. At that time the nation had only a few scattered lights to mark more than 2,000 miles of coast.

## AMERICAN LIGHTHOUSES *in* 1789

Built on Little Brewster Island near the outer edge of Boston Harbor, Boston Light (1716) was North America's first lighthouse. A cylindrical stone structure with a lantern room at the top, it set the pattern for many of the hundreds of lighthouses that would be built afterward. Destroyed in Revolutionary War raids by both Continental and British forces, it was rebuilt in 1783.

Marking the entrance to Nantucket Harbor, in Massachusetts, Brant Point Light (1746) was the second lighthouse built in the original thirteen colonies. A rather flimsy wooden structure, it burned or was blown over in storms several times only to be rebuilt by the island's tenacious whalers and fishermen, who depended on it for guidance. The Brant Point Lighthouse had burned to the ground in 1786 and had not yet been replaced at the time that Washington became president.

America's third lighthouse, Beavertail Light (1749), marked the passage into Rhode Island's Narragansett Bay. Its square, rubblestone tower anchored the southern tip of sandy Conanicut Island, which the pirate captain William Kidd had used as a hideout during the 1600s. Like the Boston Light, this one was knocked out of operation by the British during the Revolutionary War. By 1790, however, it was repaired and back in service.

Built with the proceeds of a public lottery, New London Light (1760) survived the Revolution intact. Continental privateers often used the light to help find refuge from pursuing British warships.

An octagonal brick structure, Sandy Hook Light (1764) stood near the mouth of the Hudson River and showed the way to New York City's bustling harbor. New Yorkers had financed and built this strategic light tower, but, since it was actually located in New Jersey, the legislature of the Garden State laid claim to the facility following the Revolution. This precipitated a protracted and often heated legal squabble between the two states. The matter was settled only when Congress took control of this and other U.S. lighthouses in 1789 (see pages 37–38).

Guiding ships into Delaware Bay and the river beyond, Cape Henlopen Light (1765) was one of the most important navigational markers in America. For sea captains caught in a storm, the light was a particularly welcome sight, as it marked one of the few safe harbors along the entire Eastern Seaboard. Even in the worst weather, the waters behind the cape were nearly always calm. Burned by British sailors and marines in 1777, Cape Henlopen Lighthouse was repaired and relit in 1784 (see pages 49–51).

Charleston Light (1767), located on sandy Morris Island, which was frequently inundated by high tides, pointed the way to the harbor of one of North America's oldest and most gracious cities. For decades it was the only significant navigational light south of the Virginia capes.

Serving the famed Massachusetts community founded by the Pilgrims, Plymouth Light (1768) was unique in that it displayed not one but two lights from the same building. The twin beacons set the light apart from ordinary lanterns marking nearby harbors.

During its early years Portsmouth Light (1771) consisted of little more than a lantern hoisted up the flag-pole of Fort William and Mary, on the banks of New Hampshire's Piscataqua River. In 1775 the keeper felt free temporarily to set aside his duties and take a wagonload of gunpowder to the embattled Massachusetts Minutemen on Bunker Hill. A proper wood-frame lighthouse was eventually built here. During the 1780s it received a pair of famous visitors: the Revolutionary War hero General Marquis de Lafayette and his old commander, George Washington himself.

Built to warn mariners away from Thacher Island, a barren, ship-killing rock off the north coast of Massachusetts, Cape Ann Light (1771) consisted of two separate towers. The island was named for a colonial clergyman and his family shipwrecked here in 1635. The station's first keeper was a notorious Tory. When the Revolution broke out, a party of Massachusetts militiamen hustled him off the island, plunging the twin lights into darkness until after the war.

The second lighthouse to be established on tiny Nantucket, Great Point Light (1784) stood at the northern end of the island. Although it was built of wood like the neighboring Brant Point Lighthouse, it proved more durable. It had stood for five years by the time the federal government took control of the nation's lighthouses.

Intended to guide ships safely over the treacherous sandbar at the harbor entrance, Newburyport Light (1788) was the first known use of a range-light system. Two lights were displayed, one higher and some distance behind the other. The lights appeared in perpendicular alignment only to ships in safe water.

## THE UNITED STATES LIGHTHOUSE SERVICE

Anxious to encourage commerce, President Washington recognized that the new nation's system of coastal lights was woefully inadequate. Under pressure from the president, Congress made lighthouses a priority and, in one of its very first official acts, created the United States Lighthouse Service. In one form or another, the service would survive for more than 150 years, right up until the U.S. Coast Guard took full responsibility for the nation's navigational aids in 1939. By that time nearly one thousand fine lighthouses marked the Atlantic and Gulf coasts in the East, the Pacific and Bering Sea coasts in the West, and the shores of the Great Lakes in the Midwest.

A century and a half earlier, however, when the Lighthouse Service was in its infancy, the number of operational lights was pitifully small, including only the eleven functional lights described above (the Brant Point Lighthouse was out of service at that time). To remedy this, the service undertook a major construction program that added a dozen major lights during the 1790s, the nation's first full decade of independence. These were the lighthouses at Cape Henry, Virginia (completed in 1791); Portland Head, Maine (1791); Tybee, Georgia (1791); Seguin, Maine (1795); Bald Head, North Carolina (1796); Montauk Point, New York (1797); Baker's Island, Massachusetts (1798); Cape Cod, Massachusetts (1798); Cape Hatteras, North Carolina (1798); Ocracoke, North Carolina (1798); Gay Head, Massachusetts (1799); and Eatons Neck, New York (1799).

Perhaps appropriately, this initial burst of lighthouse construction was completed shortly before George Washington died during the final weeks of 1799. The old general missed by only seventeen days witnessing the beginning of the nineteenth century and, with it, the opening of a whole new era of expansion and prosperity. As a revolutionary, signer of the Declaration of Independence, leader of the Continental Army, framer of the Constitution, and the nation's first president, Washington had done more than almost any American to make this new and optimistic age possible. Among his most important contributions, however, was one that is not frequently recognized: his insistence on an efficient system of lights for America's coasts and navigable inland waters.

*The grand Montauk Point Lighthouse marks the eastern extremity of New York's Long Island. For two centuries it has welcomed vessels and sailors emerging from the North Atlantic. Nowadays, it also welcomes many curious visitors and excited children.*

# THE LIBERTY LIGHTS

Lighthouses make navigation easier and safer, but they also serve as symbols, both profound and practical, welcoming sailors from other lands to our shores. For many of the millions of immigrants who came to America in search of opportunity and a better life, the first glimpse of their new home was the beacon of a distant lighthouse. Likely, the light most often seen first by approaching immigrants was that of the Montauk Point Lighthouse, built in 1797 at the far end of Long Island. For others it may have been the Boston Lighthouse, the Cape Hatteras Lighthouse on North Carolina's Outer Banks, the Cape Henry or Cape Charles lighthouses at the entrance of the Chesapeake Bay, or any one of dozens of other prominent coastal lights.

America's most widely known symbol of freedom is, of course, the Statue of Liberty. Striking a bold pose on the island near the entrance to the New York City Harbor, the statue has welcomed visitors and immigrants to America for more than a century. With its bright lantern thrusting more than 300 feet above the water, the statue was intended to serve as a lighthouse. For many years it was recognized as an official harbor light, useful to vessels moving up and down the Hudson River or headed for the city wharves.

Known officially as the "Statue of Liberty Enlightening the World," it was the dream of a nineteenth-century French historian named Edouard de Laboulaye, a passionate admirer of American political institutions. Laboulaye raised money for the project in France, hired Frederic Auguste Bartholdi to design the statue, and, when it was completed in 1884, presented it to the United States as a gesture of French–American friendship. The dismantled statue arrived in New York in 214 enormous packing crates. Reassembled on twelve-acre Bedloe Island, now known as Liberty Island, it was dedicated in 1886 by President Grover Cleveland.

The statue appears today almost exactly as it did more than a century ago, but it has required continual maintenance and care. During its centennial in 1986, it received a multimillion-dollar renovation, which included replacement of the 1,600 wrought-iron bands that hold the copper skin to its iron frame.

The statue weighs approximately 450,000 pounds. From her heel to the top of her head, the lady stands 111 feet tall. Her toenails are more than a foot across.

Her most heroic quality, however, is not her extraordinary size but, rather, the very powerful idea she represents. A symbol recognized the world over, she is freedom's lighthouse. Perhaps the Emma Lazarus poem engraved on a tablet at the statue's base conveys this message best. It reads:

*Not like the brazen giant of Greek fame,*

*With conquering limbs astride from land to land;*

*Here at our sea-washed, sunset gates shall stand*

*A mighty woman with a torch, whose flame*

*Is the imprisoned lightning, and her name*

*Mother of Exiles. From her beacon-hand*

*Glows world-wide welcome; her mild eyes command*

*The air-bridged harbor that twin cities frame.*

*"Keep ancient lands, your storied pomp!" cries she*

*With silent lips. "Give me your tired, your poor,*

*Your huddled masses yearning to breathe free,*

*The wretched refuse of your teeming shore.*

*Send these, the homeless, tempest-tost to me,*

*I lift my lamp beside the golden door!"*

When its temporary beacon first shined late in the year 1826, the Stony Point Lighthouse became the government's first operational light on the Hudson River. Its final lighting apparatus, installed in 1902, was a fourth-order Fresnel used previously at the Tarrytown Lighthouse. Erected some twenty miles south of West Point, Stony Point's twenty-four-foot structure housed a light that could be seen nearly twenty-two miles south along the river. Replaced by a skeleton tower in 1925, the original lighthouse now stands high on a promontory in a beautiful state park. (© William Kaufhold)

# RACE ROCK LIGHT

*Race Rock, near Fishers Island, New York – 1879*

Although it is positioned only about five miles from Watch Hill, Rhode Island, and less than eight miles from New London, Connecticut, the Race Rock Lighthouse is actually located in the state of New York. It stands on a high stone pier near where three state boundaries come together just off the tip of New York's Fishers Island.

Built at great expense and through almost superhuman effort during the late 1870s, the lighthouse marks an extraordinarily dangerous shoal known as Race Point Reef. Strong currents rushing back and forth between Long Island Sound and the Atlantic make this area a nightmare for sailors. Mariners long ago gave it the nickname the "horse race." They had a name for the reef as well: "killer."

*Built in open water atop a massive concrete pier, the Race Rock Lighthouse took eight years and several substantial federal appropriations to complete. It warns ships away from a deadly shoal near the entrance to Long Island Sound.* (Courtesy Bob and Sandra Shanklin)

A long list of ships have come to grief on Fishers Island and the nearby coasts of Connecticut and Rhode Island, but Race Point Reef itself is particularly vicious. During the 1700s and early 1800s, the reef sank ships at a rate of nearly one per year. In 1829 alone the reef claimed at least eight ships, and there likely were other wrecks that went unreported.

In 1838 Congress appropriated $3,000 to build a lighthouse on Race Rock, but this sum was so pitifully inadequate that construction was put on hold indefinitely. Meanwhile the carnage continued. Perhaps the worst disaster occured in 1846, when the passenger steamer *Atlantic* slammed into Race Point Reef, with a loss of fifty-seven lives. Despite this calamity, it was not until 1869 that Congress finally appropriated a more realistic sum, $90,000, to build the lighthouse.

But even this—at the time quite substantial funding— would prove insufficient. Before the Race Rock light station was complete, its price tag would balloon to $278,716, placing it, comparatively speaking, among the most expensive lighthouses ever built. It was also one of the most remarkable engineering feats of its era.

Construction of a lighthouse in the open waters of Long Island Sound proved a daunting task. To attempt it federal officials employed F. Hopkinson Smith, a well-known construction engineer, to bring the project to fruition. Smith in turn hired as his foreman Thomas Scott, a sharp-tongued former ship's captain whom he described as a "bifurcated sea dog." The work began in 1871, and before it was completed more than eight years later, Scott

would employ every foul phrase he had learned as a sailor and, no doubt, would invent some more.

First a pier had to be constructed in thirteen feet of often turbulent water. To this purpose, Smith and Scott tried building an artificial island by dumping tons of stone onto Race Rock. Enormous loads of broken rocks and boulders—10,000 tons in all—were poured onto the site, but the strong currents swept away the fill almost as fast as boats could deliver it. Frustrated, Smith and Scott resorted to the much slower and more expensive method of having divers lay cement on the sea bottom. This process took nearly two years but eventually produced a mass of concrete some nine feet thick and sixty-nine feet in diameter. Upon this pad they were able to construct a stone pier.

The job was still far from finished. Progress was impeded by storms, ice, sunken supply barges, exhausted funding, appropriation delays, and the death of two workmen in separate accidents. In all, it took almost a decade to complete the pier and lighthouse. It was not until February 21, 1879, that a keeper climbed the steps of the tower and lit the lamps for the first time. Nonetheless, mariners fighting the five-knot currents of the "horse race" were glad enough to see it.

Built of large granite blocks, the two-story Race Rock Lighthouse stands on a massive stone pier rising almost thirty feet above high water. The attached square tower places the light approximately sixty-seven feet above the surface of Long Island Sound. The automated light alternates between red and white flashes and can be seen from fourteen miles away.

## HOW TO GET THERE:

While the Race Rock Lighthouse can be reached only by water, its light can be seen from Watch Hill, Rhode Island, and several points along the Connecticut coast. The ferries from New London, Connecticut, to Orient Point, New York, and Block Island, Rhode Island, often pass within sight of Race Rock. The ferries operate only during the summer. For prices and schedules call (203) 442–9553. Incidentally, New London, Watch Hill, and Block Island have delightful lighthouses of their own, all worth a visit (see New England Lighthouses, The Globe Pequot Press, 1996).

# MONTAUK POINT LIGHT

*Long Island, New York – 1797*

The prominent bluff at the far eastern extremity of Long Island reminded early European settlers of the hump in a turtle's back, so they called the place Turtle Hill. But the unpretentious name belies the importance of this strategic point of land.

Long before the arrival of the white man, the first beacons burned on the hill known to Indians as Womponamon. According to legend, leaders of the powerful Montauk tribe lit signal fires at the summit of the hill to call their chiefs and warriors to council. The vessels guided by this light were dugout canoes carved from the trunks of large trees.

Some say that the British also banked bright fires on the hill. During the Revolutionary War several of King George's ships lay off Montauk Point in order to blockade Long Island Sound. The fires served these warships as beacons.

After the war the new United States government recognized that it must follow the example of the British and the

*The Montauk tower looms above its dwelling, now a museum and visitors center. The erosion that, until recently, threatened to dump the two-century-old structure into the Atlantic has been stopped.*

Indians before them. Such a significant and dangerous headland could not be left unmarked, and President George Washington himself ordered construction of a lighthouse on Montauk Point. It was to be an expensive project. Contractor John McComb of New York submitted a low bid of $22,300 to dig foundations, haul sandstone, and build the tower and two-story keeper's dwelling. At a time when lighthouses elsewhere were being built for as little as $2,000, this was a hefty price. Land for the light station had been purchased for only a little more than $250. But McComb gave the country its money's worth. He built the lighthouse like a fortress, with a foundation thirteen feet deep and walls seven feet thick at the base. As a consequence, the Montauk Point Lighthouse still stands after almost two centuries of blasting by Atlantic storms. McComb was also the contractor for a lighthouse erected in 1791 on Cape Henry in Virginia. The tower he built there, though unused for more than a century, stands to this day.

Generations of immigrants caught their first sight of America at Montauk Point, and the lighthouse there became for many of them a symbol of the freedom and opportunity waiting for them in their new country. That the old light tower should fall is unthinkable; it would be as jarring as if someone chiseled the faces off the side of Mount Rushmore or bowled over the Statue of Liberty.

The Montauk Point Lighthouse continues to guide ships 200 years after its lamps first burned. Not all of the sailors who have seen the light, however, have reached port safely. Storms have driven many vessels against the beaches near Montauk, usually with disastrous results. Some ships got permanently stuck in the sand, others broke in half and sank, and a few "melted like a lump of sugar" in the raging surf. More than a century ago, local residents told a correspondent for *Harper's New Monthly* magazine about "how a ship was driven ashore one wild night . . . how brave men gathered to the rescue; how the crew, one after another dropped into the sea, some of them being saved from the jaws of the angry waves; of a mother washed ashore, dead, clasping a babe in her arms; the wild figures of the wreckers on that dark, stormy night of horrors, lit up by a great fire of drift-wood. . . . "

Ships are not the only wrecks found on the Montauk beaches. Whales occasionally end their days there as well. For reasons that are still not understood, whales sometimes beach themselves on the shores of Long Island (and elsewhere). Unless they can be coaxed or winched back into the ocean, they die. Long Island settlers and, no doubt, the Indians before them were quite familiar with the phenomenon of beached whales. The first pastor of

*Years ago, this double-lamp, airport-style lighting system replaced a first-order Fresnel lens at Montauk.*

the church at East Hampton, a few miles from Montauk, received as his salary "forty-five pounds annually, lands rate free, grain to be first ground at the mill every Monday, and one-fourth of the whales stranded on the beach."

For many decades the lamps of the lighthouse at Montauk Point burned whale oil, though it was a commercial variety and was not taken from the unfortunate animals that happened onto nearby beaches. By the mid-1850s whalers had decimated the world's whale population. Seeing that it could no longer count on a regular supply of whale oil, the Lighthouse Service switched to lard oil as a fuel here and elsewhere. Later many lighthouse lamps, including those at Montauk, burned kerosene.

## HOW TO GET THERE:

Follow Route 27 to Montauk Point State Park, at the far eastern end of Long Island. If you could visit only one lighthouse in America, the Montauk Light would be a good choice. The museum in the old keeper's dwelling displays an outstanding collection of nautical and lighthouse artifacts, including several classic Fresnel lenses. The museum is well worth the small admission charge, which goes toward preservation of the lighthouse.

# ORIENT POINT LIGHT

*Orient Point, New York – 1899*

Just off the northeastern tip of Long Island, a deep but narrow passage called Plum Gut links several heavily trafficked bodies of water, including Long Island Sound and Gardiners Bay. Strong currents make navigating any part of the Gut a tricky business. But a helmsman's chief concern is Oyster Pond Reef, a deadly ledge lurking just beneath the surface of the water and extending fully one third of the way across the waterway.

To mark this unseen menace, in 1896 the Lighthouse Board approved construction of a caisson-type tower in the open water at the far end of the reef. The Orient Point Lighthouse took two years to build and was not operational until 1899. It cost $30,000, about six times the original estimate for the project. To protect the structure from high waves driven by gales, the builders piled hundreds of tons of broken stone around its base. Painted brown at the top and white at the bottom, the cast-iron tower was not particularly handsome. It was soon given the nickname "Coffee Pot" by mariners who passed regularly through Plum Gut.

The station's first keeper was N. A. Anderson, a Norwegian immigrant. He was married, but because his isolated light station was considered too small and dangerous for a woman, his wife lived in the town of Orient on Long Island. Anderson served for twenty years in the Coffee Pot at a salary of $50 a month.

Now unmanned and automated, the Orient Point Light guides maritime traffic with a white flash every five seconds. The tower stands sixty-four feet above the water, and its light can be seen for fifteen miles.

## HOW TO GET THERE:

The lighthouse cannot be reached by land but can be seen from Orient Point. It can also be seen from the ferry connecting New London, Connecticut, and Orient Point. For ferry schedules, fares, and other information, call (860) 442–9553.

Located off Fishers Island near Orient Point, New York, the 81-foot granite tower of the Little Gull Island Lighthouse dates to 1869. Its powerful, second-order Fresnel lens is still is use. The station is closed to the public. (Courtesy Bob and Sandra Shanklin)

# HORTON POINT LIGHT

*Southold, New York – 1790 and 1857*

In 1757, during the French and Indian War, a young military officer from Virginia paused atop one of the high bluffs of Southold, New York, and gazed thoughtfully down onto Long Island Sound. He had come here to see firsthand a notorious stretch of coast known to locals and to the survivors of no few shipwrecks as "Dead Man's Cove." The Virginian told his companions that someday a lighthouse would be built on the very spot where he was standing. His name was George Washington, and many years later, in 1790, while serving as the nation's first president, he would commission the lighthouse himself.

In June 1990 the Horton Point Lighthouse celebrated the 200th anniversary of its commissioning. The event, attended by dignitaries and many friends of the old lighthouse, was doubly significant. On that same day the light was restored to active service after standing dark for fifty-eight years, the Coast Guard having decommissioned the lighthouse in 1933.

The Horton Point Lighthouse seen today was built on the bluffs during the mid-1850s. In June 1857, a century after Washington first visited the place, the whale-oil lamps were lit and the third-order Fresnel lamp began to throw light out over the Sound.

From 1903 to 1904 Stella Prince served as keeper of the Horton Point Light. Born and raised in the lighthouse itself, she was the daughter of an earlier keeper. Appointed by President Theodore Roosevelt, she was one of only a few women ever to receive an official appointment as a lighthouse keeper.

## HOW TO GET THERE:

*From Route 25 or Route 48 in Southold, follow Horton Lane toward Long Island Sound. Turn right onto Sound View Road and then left onto Lighthouse Road. The Southold Historical Society operates a delightful nautical museum at the lighthouse. Hours are 11:30 A.M.–4:00 P.M. on Saturday and Sunday during summer months. For more specific information or for special tours, call (516) 765–3262.*

(© William Kaufhold)

Built in 1868, the Cedar Island Lighthouse served the old whaling community of Sag Harbor, near the eastern tip of Long Island. The two-story granite dwelling and forty-foot tower replaced an earlier lighthouse in operation here since 1839. The station was abandoned in 1934, when a nearby skeleton tower was completed. Local historical organizations hope to restore the original structure to its former glory. (Courtesy Bob and Sandra Shanklin)

# FIRE ISLAND LIGHT

*Fire Island, New York – 1826 and 1858*

In 1850 the SS *Elizabeth* struck the sandy shoals off the south coast of Long Island and sank almost within sight of the Fire Island Light station. Ironically, the ship's captain had been looking for the light when he hit the shoals. Many of the *Elizabeth*'s crew drowned, and the disaster precipitated a public outcry. Mariners complained that the seventy-four-foot Fire Island tower, built in 1826, was far too short to accomplish its task of warning sailors away from the shoals.

Although Congress quickly appropriated money to rebuild the lighthouse and raise the height of the tower,

nothing was done until 1857, when construction began at last. By that time the Lighthouse Board had launched a major effort to revamp the nation's sadly deteriorated system of navigational lights. Some lighthouses were repointed and repaired, while others were pulled down and replaced altogether. Lantern rooms all along the Eastern Seaboard received improved lamps and the marvelously effective Fresnel lenses made in Paris.

The plan for Fire Island included a new tower nearly twice as high as the original. When masons laid the last brick on the tower during the fall of 1858, it stood 180 feet above the ground. A steel circular staircase with 192 steps led to the lantern room. The low, sandy island gave the tower a boost of about seventeen feet, so the station's new Fresnel lens flashed its message to ships at sea from a point 197 feet above the water.

The Lighthouse Board long considered the Fire Island Light one of its most important light stations. Because of its flashing characteristic, the light is known affectionately to many as "Winking Woman."

## HOW TO GET THERE:

*The light can be reached by road from West Islip or by ferry from Bay Shore. The light stands high above the low, sandy barrier island. Once on the island, just head toward the lighthouse; you can't miss it. The Fire Island Preservation Society has restored and relit the old 1858 light, installed an interpretive center in the living quarters, and established a foundation to maintain the station.*

*Decommissioned by the Coast Guard, Fire Island Light went dark in 1974. But it burns brightly again now, thanks to the efforts of a local preservation society. (© William Kaufhold)*

The Old Field Point Lighthouse, near Stony Brook, New York, marks one of several fingers of land that push forward from Long Island and menace shipping in Long Island Sound. Built of granite in 1823, the tower is thirty-five feet high. Its fourth-order Fresnel lens was recently replaced by an airport-style beacon. The grounds are open to the public and can be reached via Old Field Road off Main Street in Stony Brook. (Courtesy Bob and Sandra Shanklin)

# EATONS NECK LIGHT

*Asharoken, New York – 1799*

One of only a handful of surviving eighteenth-century light towers, the Eatons Neck Lighthouse near Asharoken on Long Island remains in operation today after nearly 200 years of service. Established to guide ships into Huntington Bay and through the western reaches of Long Island Sound, it was completed in 1799, during the administration of John Adams, the nation's second president.

Like many early lighthouses, this one was built with fieldstone, most of it gathered locally. Even so, time has proven the work remarkably sound. To supervise construction of the tower and dwelling, the government hired John McComb, who also served as contractor for the Montauk Point and Cape Henry lighthouses. Obviously, McComb built structures intended to last, as these two towers and the seventy-foot octagonal tower at Eatons Neck still stand after two centuries of storm, rain, and wind. The Eatons Neck Lighthouse received substantial repairs and renovation in 1868. Otherwise, it has required only minor patching and fixing and remains today essentially the same structure that McComb built in 1799.

Originally equipped with only a simple oil lamp, the lantern displayed a weak light visible from just a few miles out into the sound. Eventually, the station was fitted with an Argand lamp and reflector system designed by Winslow Lewis. The highly polished, thirteen-inch reflectors provided a more powerful light, but the Lewis system was decidedly inferior to the Fresnel lenses manufactured by the French. For many years Fifth Auditor Stephen Pleasonton of the Treasury Department resisted adoption of the Fresnel system because of the high cost of the hand-polished glass lenses—and, some would say, because of his preference for Lewis. (By the time Eatons Neck Lighthouse received its third-order Fresnel in 1856, Pleasonton was no longer head of the U.S. Lighthouse Establishment.)

Since this area is frequently blanketed by fog, early Eatons Neck keepers spent many hours striking the station's bell. During the 1868 renovation the bell was replaced by a siren. In 1904 an automated foghorn took over the task of warning fog-blinded mariners.

Although the station is still used as a dwelling by Coast Guard personnel, the light itself is automated. Since the tower stands on a bank nearly equal to its own height, the light shines from a lofty 140 feet above the waters of the sound.

(Courtesy Bob and Sandra Shanklin)

## HOW TO GET THERE:

On Long Island follow Route 26A through Cold Spring Harbor and Centerport, then turn left at the sign for Asharoken and Eatons Neck. The lighthouse is located at the very end of Lighthouse Road.

# CONEY ISLAND LIGHT

*Brooklyn, New York – 1890*

A blue-collar lighthouse if ever there was one, the sturdy, steel skeleton tower on Coney Island was assigned the task of guiding New York City garbage barges to their watery dumps several miles out into the Atlantic. Built in 1890, the lighthouse also guided hulking iron freighters to Coney Island loading docks.

The sixty-eight-foot Coney Island tower consists of a central steel cylinder topped by an enclosed platform, which, in turn, is crowned by the gallery and lantern room. The entire structure is braced by four steel legs arranged to form a pyramid.

Originally, the Coney Island Lighthouse was the rear member of a pair of range lights marking a safe channel for the garbage scows. The front range light was taken out of service shortly before the turn of the century, but the rear range light remains in service to this day. It displays a flashing red light.

## HOW TO GET THERE:

From I–278 follow the Prospect Parkway and Ocean Parkway to Coney Island. The lighthouse is located on Surf Avenue between Forty-sixth and Forty-seventh streets. Coney Island, which can also be reached by subway (recommended for the adventurous only), abounds in attractions, including the New York City Aquarium and the famous Coney Island Beach.

*The skeleton-style tower of the Coney Island Lighthouse lifts its lantern above the homes of an old Brooklyn neighborhood.* (Courtesy U.S. Coast Guard)

# LIGHTSHIP *AMBROSE*

*New York City, New York – 1907*

America's once-proud fleet of lightships has been retired, but for many years these little vessels guided ships and marked obstacles in remote areas that even the most powerful lighthouse beacons could not reach. They remained anchored at their duty stations, often for months at a time. Equipment failures, ice floes—even hurricanes could not knock them off their posts for long.

Among the sturdiest of these floating lighthouses was the lightship *Ambrose*. Built in the Camden, New Jersey, shipyards in 1907, it served at one duty station for more than sixty years. Christened with the rather unpoetical name *Lightship No. 87*, its first assignment was in the Ambrose Channel, leading to New York City. On station there for nearly a quarter of a century, it became known to passing sailors and lightship crewmen as the *Ambrose*.

Only 135 feet long and with a beam of 29 feet, the 680-ton *Ambrose* was tiny compared to the huge freighters and passenger liners passing back and forth through the channel. On several occasions it was hit by much larger vessels, but it always survived.

In 1932 it was pulled off the Ambrose Channel station and relegated to service as a relief lightship. In 1936, however, the *Ambrose* was reassigned to the crucial Scotland station just off Sandy Hook, New Jersey, where it served until 1964. That year the old lightship went into semiretirement and was given the honor of representing the U.S. Coast Guard as an exhibit at the 1964 New York World's Fair.

Since 1968 the *Ambrose* has delighted children and fascinated adults as a key attraction of the South Street Seaport Museum in New York City. The *Ambrose* is a maritime exhibit of particular historical interest. Originally, the lamps atop its main mast and foremast were lit with oil and its engines powered by steam. Eventually, its lamps were converted to electricity and its engines to diesel power.

## HOW TO GET THERE:

*By car, follow FDR Drive on Manhattan's East Side to the Brooklyn Bridge and Civic Center exit, which will place you on Water and Pearl streets, just 3 blocks north of the South Street Seaport Museum. From the West Side drive around the southern toe of Manhattan through the Battery Park underpass to South Street and the museum. The museum complex is open daily all year long. Admission is charged for most exhibits, including the* Ambrose. *For hours, special events, and other information, call (212) 732–7678 or (212) 669–9400.*

Lightship Number 87 *heads for the Ambrose Channel leading to New York City. Reaching its appointed station, the little lighthouse would drop anchor and maintain its lonely vigil for months at a time. Notice the lantern held aloft by a tripod-type mast. Nowadays, the* Ambrose *is a popular attraction of the South Street Seaport Museum in New York City.* (Courtesy U.S. Coast Guard)

# JEFFREY'S HOOK LIGHT

*New York City, New York – 1920*

Perhaps no other port on Earth is so well lit as New York City. Soaring 1,350 feet into the night sky from the seaward toe of Manhattan Island, the twin towers of the World Trade Center can be seen from dozens of miles out in the Atlantic. A New York–bound navigator could hardly miss them or the Empire State Building, with its television tower topping out at 1,414 feet. At the harbor entrance the 300-foot Statue of Liberty (from foundation to torch), originally intended as a lighthouse, is awash in floodlight. So it is ironic that New York is home to the diminutive Jeffrey's Hook Lighthouse, known to many New Yorkers as the "little red lighthouse under the George Washington Bridge."

A steel-plated cylinder only forty feet tall, the bright red lighthouse is dwarfed by the bridge, which towers hundreds of feet overhead. Built in 1920, the small Jeffrey's Hook tower replaced a pair of simple stake lights, which had stood here since 1889. The lighthouse would serve for less than a dozen years, however, before completion of the George Washington Bridge in 1931 rendered it obsolete. The bridge's massive 3,500-foot span has special lights marking the safe channel for ships moving up and down the Hudson River.

Having lost its job to the bridge, the lighthouse appeared to be headed for oblivion. In fact, the Coast Guard intended to dismantle the metal tower and auction it off as scrap to the highest bidder. However, the publication of a now-famous children's book, *The Little Red Lighthouse and the Great Gray Bridge,* by Hildegarde Hoyt Swift, stirred up a storm of public protest. The book made the point that, even in a land of giants, "little things and little people" have a vital part to play and must be respected. Faced with a sort of children's crusade to save the lighthouse, the Coast Guard relented and deeded the structure to the New York City Parks Department. Today the Jeffrey's Hook Lighthouse survives as a much-loved attraction of New York's Fort Washington Park.

---

### HOW TO GET THERE:

The Jeffrey's Hook Lighthouse stands directly under the George Washington Bridge on the Manhattan side of the Hudson River. Take the Fort Washington exit off Manhattan's Riverside Drive.

*The little red lighthouse (Jeffrey's Hook) lies inconspicuously beneath the great gray (George Washington) bridge. (© William Kaufhold)*

R ising from a granite pier near the middle of the heavily trafficked Hudson River, Esopus Meadows Lighthouse has withstood more than a century of battering storms, high water, and winter ice floes. Built in 1879, it replaced an earlier structure that had been smashed to bits by ice. During the late 1960s the Coast Guard decommissioned the lighthouse, replacing it with a light on a nearby steel tower. Now under restoration by the Saugerties Lighthouse Conservancy, the old light station can be reached only by boat. (Courtesy Bob and Sandra Shanklin)

# KINGSTON LIGHT

*Kingston, New York – 1880 and 1915*

At a wide, sweeping bend in the Hudson River, an old lighthouse marks the harbor entrance of the inland port city of Kingston. The two-story brick dwelling and attached fifty-foot-tall tower stand near where the waters of Rondout Creek enter the river.

An earlier lighthouse built at the site in 1880 had to be replaced after a series of dikes shifted the entrance well away from the original shoreline. The existing structure, known locally as Rondout Two, was completed in 1915 and has remained in service ever since. Nearly surrounded by the waters of the Hudson and Rondout Creek, it stands on a solid concrete pier.

The Coast Guard automated the light in 1954 and in recent years replaced the original fifth-order Fresnel lens with a modern plastic device. The dwelling stood empty for more than thirty years before being leased to the Hud-son River Maritime Center for eventual use as a museum. With assistance from the City of Kingston, the interior of the dwelling has been refurbished and filled with historic exhibits, including a display on the lives of keepers and their families. The museum is open on weekends during the summer and fall.

## HOW TO GET THERE:

Kingston can be reached by way of I–87 (the New York Thruway) or Route 9. For museum hours and other information, contact the Hudson River Maritime Center (914–338–0071) or the Kingston Chamber of Commerce (914–338–5100).

*The Kingston Lighthouse, known to local residents as Rondout Two, marks a sharp bend in the Hudson River north of Pough-keepsie.* (Courtesy Bob and Sandra Shanklin)

# SAUGERTIES LIGHT

*Saugerties, New York – 1836 and 1869*

A stone lighthouse stood beside the Hudson River at Saugerties as early as 1836, but after about thirty years, time and floodwaters had damaged it beyond repair. In the late 1860s construction began on a new Saugerties lighthouse, which went into service in 1869. The two-story brick dwelling and attached tower were built on a low stone caisson only a few feet above high water (the Hudson has tides of up to four feet). The octagonal iron lantern atop the square tower contained a sixth-order—the smallest available—Fresnel lens.

Located at the confluence of Esopus Creek and the Hudson River, the Saugerties Lighthouse guided several generations of river pilots. It was finally closed in 1954, bringing to an end eighty-five years of continuous service. Afterward the Coast Guard established a new, automated light on a nearby steel tower.

Abandoned for more than twenty years, the old lighthouse fell into a sad state of disrepair and seemed on the verge of collapse. A group of concerned local citizens then formed the Saugerties Lighthouse Conservancy and set about raising money to restore the dilapidated structure. Many years of prodigious conservancy efforts have led to a handsome restoration, and the lighthouse is now open to the public as a museum.

## HOW TO GET THERE:

The town of Saugerties can be reached by way of I–87 or the more scenic Route 9. The lighthouse is open to the public on weekends during warm-weather months. For more information contact the Saugerties Lighthouse Conservancy at (914) 246–4380.

*The Saugerties Lighthouse, well maintained by a local conservancy group, guided several generations of Hudson River pilots.*
(Courtesy Bob and Sandra Shanklin)

# HUDSON CITY LIGHT

*Hudson City, New York – 1874*

It's a rare thing for a major navigational light to shine more than one hundred miles from the nearest expanse of open water. This can be said, however, of the Hudson City Lighthouse. In fact, not one but two mountain ranges, the Catskills and Berkshires, stand between this lighthouse and the sea.

Established in 1874 to mark the dangerous Middle Ground Flats near the inland port cities of Hudson and Athens, New York, the Hudson City Lighthouse still guides shipping to this day. The flats have scarred or breached the hulls of more than one river freighter and barge.

The brick dwelling and forty-eight-foot tower stand on a limestone pier that protects the structure from ice floes. The tower is topped by a small, octagonal lantern room, which once held a fifth-order Fresnel lens. Today the light is automated, and the building is maintained by a local conservation organization dedicated to preserving the old lighthouse.

While winter ice was always a threat to lighthouses and other structures along the river, it also provided seasonal employment for many hard-working laborers along this stretch of the Hudson. The thick, clear river ice was sawed into enormous blocks and stored in insulated warehouses for sale during warm-weather months. During the late nineteenth and early twentieth centuries, this Hudson River bounty kept iceboxes cold and rattled in the drink glasses of sweltering city dwellers every summer.

## HOW TO GET THERE:

*Hudson City can be reached from New York City or Albany via I–87 or Route 9. The lighthouse itself stands well out in the Hudson River and can be reached only by boat.*

*The Hudson City Lighthouse guards the dangerous Middle Ground Flats, a series of dangerous Hudson River shallows that have claimed many barges and other river vessels.* (Courtesy Bob and Sandra Shanklin)

*The 157½-foot tower of the Cape May Lighthouse rises into the evening sky. The winding staircase inside the tower has 199 steps.* (© Mark Riddick/New Light Photography)

# CHAPTER TWO

# *Lights of*
# THE LONG SANDY SHORE
## NEW JERSEY

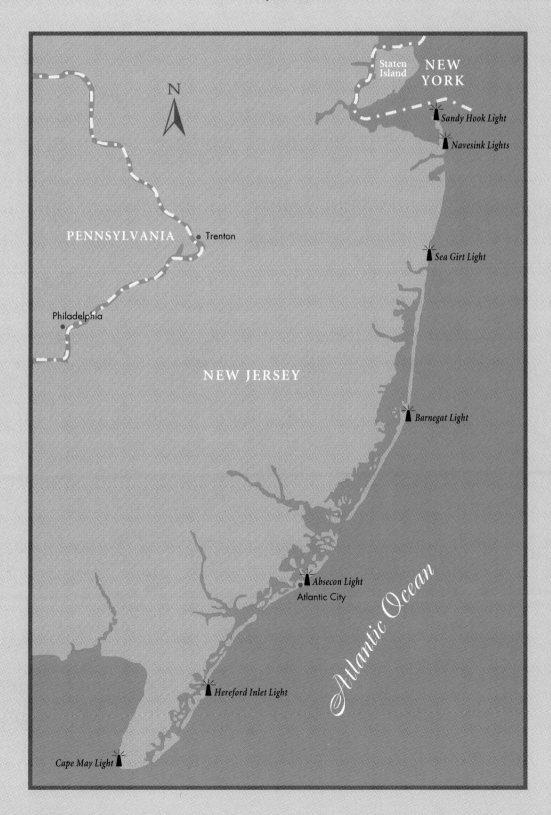

*The Barnegat Lighthouse tower stands regally above a New Jersey beach. The Barnegat Light, located forty-five miles south of Sandy Hook, was built to last in 1858. Its brick walls are ten feet thick at the base, eighteen inches thick at the top. (© William Kaufhold)*

hile the U.S. Lighthouse Service, established in 1789, struggled to improve and expand the nation's system of navigational lights, most of the country's coastline remained in the dark. Approximately two dozen lighthouses were in service by 1800, but along vast stretches of often-treacherous shoreline, ships' captains could depend only upon their own skills and instincts for guidance.

Ships nearing the coast were in especially desperate straits when caught in a gale. With no lights to guide them, crews dared not make a run for safe harbor for fear of striking a shoal or having their vessel thrown up on some low, unseen headland and pounded to pieces by breakers. Usually, their only choice was to attempt to ride out the storm. Often they and their ships were swallowed up by the sea and never heard from again.

Hurricanes and nor'easters (sometimes called "winter's hurricanes") strike the Mid-Atlantic coast frequently. During the 1800s, when there were no radar or satellites in the sky to track them, these fierce storms appeared without warning. Capable of smashing whole fleets, they often devastated shipping along several hundred miles of coast. The following is only one of the countless maritime calamities caused by these titanic storms.

## THE LAST DAYS *of the* ROSE-IN-BLOOM

On Saturday, August 16, 1806, the *Rose-in-Bloom,* a handsomely outfitted ship of commerce, set sail from Charleston, South Carolina, bound for New York City. Among the forty-nine passengers and crew were several notables, including Congressman John Rutledge and the eminent General Joseph MacPherson, who was accompanied by his daughter Eliza. Once outside the Charleston Harbor, Captain Stephen Barber, a shipmaster of many years' experience, pointed the bow of his ship confidently northward toward New York. It was a voyage he had successfully completed many times before, but this trip would not be like the others.

By the morning of Friday, August 22, the *Rose-in-Bloom* had made only modest headway and stood just to the northeast of Cape Hatteras. Captain Barber had been fighting unfavorable winds for days and was keeping an eye on the weather. He did not like what he saw—black thunderheads, streaked by lightning, were boiling up out of the southeast. By midday the gale overtook the ship, and it quickly became apparent that this was no ordinary storm.

Before long the winds had torn the sails to shreds. Captain Barber turned the bow into the wind and attempted to heave to under a lone topsail. The *Rose-in-Bloom* held its own for a time, but the topsail was soon ripped away, leaving the ship to drift and wallow helplessly in the towering waves. For nearly two days the ship was driven northward by the wind. Then, on Sunday morning, she capsized.

Trapped belowdecks, some of the passengers and crew perished immediately. Others scrambled out through gangways, portholes, and skylights to take refuge on the hull. Eventually, muscular crewmen were able to cut away the masts with axes, and the ship slowly righted itself. But the *Rose-in-Bloom* was now a shattered hulk, little better than a raft. Heavy seas constantly swept over the deck, carrying away the weak or unwary. Passenger Benjamin Booth had his wife and infant son torn from his arms and washed into the sea. During the night General MacPherson died of cold and exposure. As he died MacPherson begged Congressman Rutledge to save his daugher Eliza. But no one on the broken ship thought that they would ever see land again.

losing commerce to better-marked harbors at Boston and elsewhere, a group of New York merchants petitioned their colonial council for a lighthouse. The New York Assembly then held a lottery to raise money and hired Isaac Conro to build a tower near the mouth of the Hudson. To defray the costs of maintenance and pay the keeper's salary, the assembly levied a tax of twenty-two pence per ton on ships arriving at the Port of New York.

When completed, Conro's handiwork was described as follows: "This House is of an Octogan Figure, having eight equal sides; the Diameter of the Base 29 feet; and at the Top of the Wall 15 feet. The Lanthorn is 7 feet high; the Circumference 15 feet. The whole Construction of the Lanthorn is Iron; the Top covered with Copper. There are 48 Oil Blazes. The Building from the Surface is Nine Stories; the whole from Bottom to Top 103 feet." The dimensions of the tower remain roughly the same today.

After the Revolution the Sandy Hook Light precipitated a different sort of war. Since the lighthouse was located in New Jersey but owned by New York, the two states fell into a heated dispute over control of the station.

The verbal and legal squabbling continued for years, until the U.S. government finally put an end to the almost-comical conflict in 1790 by making the Sandy Hook station and other lighthouses a federal responsibility.

When the Lighthouse Board began its massive effort during the 1850s to rebuild and modernize America's outdated light stations, inspectors were sent to see if the Sandy Hook tower would need to be replaced. Their report on the board is a compliment to the work done by Conro almost a century earlier: "The tower at Sandy Hook main light was constructed in 1764 under royal charter, of rubblestone, and is now in a good state of preservation. Neither leaks nor cracks were observed in it. The mortar appeared to be good, and it was stated that the annual repairs upon this tower amount to a smaller sum than in towers of any of the minor lights in the New York District."

The board did decide to replace the reflectors in the lantern with a third-order Fresnel lens. Its focal plane eighty-eight feet above the water, the old lens still guides ships into the Hudson with a fixed white light visible from about nineteen miles away.

## HOW TO GET THERE:

Take Route 36 to Highlands Beach, enter Sandy Hook National Park, and follow the signs to the lighthouse. Still owned and maintained by the Coast Guard, the lighthouse can be approached for viewing. For current information call the Sandy Hook National Park at (908) 872–0115.

# NAVESINK (TWIN LIGHTS) LIGHTS

*Highlands, New Jersey – 1828 and 1862*

The twin rubblestone towers atop the Navesink Highlands, just south of Sandy Hook, stand among the most historic lighthouses in America. Navigational lights shined from this bold headland for almost two centuries, and uncounted thousands of mariners owe the safety of their ships and their very lives to the guidance that these lights provided.

Rising some 200 feet above sea level, the highlands themselves have always served as a natural daymark. Long before the first lights were established here during the mid-1700s, the hills were observed and noted in the logs of European explorers who passed along what is now the northern New Jersey coast. One such adventurous navigator was Henry Hudson, who sailed his ship *Half-Moon* out of the misty waters off Sandy Hook Bay on September 2, 1609. Hudson and his crew saw a series of "high hills" rising from the mists. When the weather cleared enough for them to move in for a closer look, they discovered "a very good land to fall with and a pleasant land to see."

Many others also found these lands pleasant, as New Jersey and New York grew into prosperous colonies, with bustling ports near the mouth of the Hudson River. To

*The fortresslike appearance of Navesink Lighthouse belies its peaceful mission. The twin-towered light station guided freighter traffic in and out of the Hudson River from 1828 until 1953.* (Courtesy U.S. Coast Guard)

protect these ports from raids by enemy fleets, the colonists established an early warning station at Navesink. Whenever a likely hostile fleet was sighted, a beacon was lighted to alert colonists and their militia as far away as New York City. Ironically, the first Navesink lighthouse was meant as a warning to landward folk rather than to ships and seamen.

A true navigational light is believed to have been in operation here as early as 1756. The light is mentioned in some documents dating to the Revolutionary War, but little else is known about it.

With American independence came a burgeoning of shipping traffic in and out of the Hudson. To help guide these ships, the Navesink Lighthouse was built in 1828. A matched pair of stone towers standing 320 feet apart placed the focal plane of the two lights more than 240 feet above sea level.

Government officials considered this to be among the best and most useful light stations in the country. In fact, the Navesink station was considered so important to maritime commerce that the nation's first Fresnel lenses were installed in its towers. In 1838 Commodore Matthew Perry sailed for France, where he purchased a pair of the advanced prismatic lenses (one first order and one second order) and had them shipped to America. By 1841 the big Fresnels were shining powerfully from the twin Navesink towers.

Several other firsts were associated with the Navesink Lighthouse. It was the first in America to have lamps fueled by kerosene (1883). The first electrically powered seacoast light shined from the south tower beginning in 1898. (By that time an electric navigational light was already in use at the Statue of Liberty, but it served only as a harbor light.)

In 1899 the Navesink Highlands became the site of another first that had profound significance for navigation and for human progress. Employing a transmitter and mast located not far from the light station, Guglielmo Marconi conducted the first practical demonstration of his wireless telegraph. Using the air rather than a wire to carry the electronic dots and dashes, Marconi relayed the results of the America's Cup races off Sandy Hook.

The fortresslike brownstone towers seen today at Navesink date to 1861: They replaced the earlier structure at the beginning of the American Civil War. By 1898 the government no longer saw a need for two lights here. It snuffed out the lamp in the north tower. The powerful south light, which could be seen from twenty-two miles at sea, served until 1953, when it, too, was discontinued.

*The north tower of the Navesink Lighthouse remained in service until 1953.*

Today the station is part of Twin Lights Historic Site, administered by the New Jersey State Park Service.

### HOW TO GET THERE:

To reach the Twin Lights Historic Site, take exit 117 off the Garden State Parkway and follow Highway 36 to Highlands and the museum parking lot. A small Fresnel lens can be seen at the museum, which features displays recounting the rich history of the station. Museum hours are from 10:00 A.M. until dusk daily. During the winter the museum is closed on Mondays and Tuesdays.

# SEA GIRT LIGHT

*Sea Girt, New Jersey – 1896*

With its weathered brick walls, pitched roof, and spacious balustered porch, the Sea Girt Lighthouse looks much like the other homes and summer cottages in this seaside community. Unlike neighboring houses, however, this one wraps around two sides of a square, forty-foot tower with a gallery and small lantern room perched on top.

Now operated as a private aid to navigation, this homey looking lighthouse was built in 1896 to guide fishing boats and other vessels into the shallow Sea Girt Inlet. The light also filled in a dark stretch along the coast between Barnegat Lighthouse, twenty-six miles to the south, and the twin Navesink Lights, some nineteen miles north. The lighthouse accomplished its tasks with a fourth-order Fresnel lens displaying a flashing red light.

In 1917 the Lighthouse Service began experimenting with radio beacons to help guide ships in fog and stormy weather. A pair of transmitters on the New York area lightships *Ambrose* and *Fire Island* and a third at Sea Girt enable navigators to pinpoint their locations through a process of triangulation. The system was eventually adopted worldwide.

A radio beacon would have done little to help the cruise ship *Morro Castle*, which caught fire on September 8, 1934, just off the New Jersey coast at Sea Girt. The intense flames prevented many of the 562 passengers and crew from reaching the ship's lifeboats, forcing them either to perish on ship or to jump into the sea. In all, 134 lives were lost to the flames or to drowning. Some of the survivors found temporary refuge in the Sea Girt Lighthouse and in nearby homes.

The Coast Guard discontinued the Sea Girt Light in 1945 and sold the property to the town. During the 1980s the building was handsomely restored, with funds raised by the Sea Girt Lighthouse Citizens Committee.

## HOW TO GET THERE:

*From the Garden State Parkway just south of I–195, take the Highway 34 exit and drive south for approximately 6 miles. Then take Route 71 north to Sea Girt. The lighthouse is located at the corner of Beach Boulevard and Ocean Road in a pleasant residential neighborhood. Visitors are welcome.*

(© William Kaufhold)

# BARNEGAT LIGHT

*Long Beach Island, New Jersey – 1835 and 1859*

The man who built the first lighthouse on New Jersey's Barnegat Inlet was none other than Winslow Lewis, a key figure in the early history of the American lighthouse establishment. A retired sea caption, Lewis held a patent on the Argand lamp and parabolic reflector system used in many American lighthouse until the 1850s. A friend of Treasury Department fifth auditor and lighthouse czar Stephen Pleasonton, Lewis often won contracts to build and equip light stations.

Lewis's forty-five-foot Barnegat Inlet tower stood for only about twenty years before a Lighthouse Board inspector found it to be poorly constructed, in a woeful state of disrepair, and hopelessly inadequate for service as a seacoast light. In truth, the board did not think much of Lewis's reflectors, either; it was busy replacing hundreds of them with the vastly more effective Fresnel lenses made by the French.

The inspector who gave the light its bad report was Lieutenant George Meade. The lieutenant found that Lewis had used decidedly inferior materials in the tower. Mortar crumbled from between bricks, and just below the lantern, a wall bulged out and seemed about to fall. Even if it were repaired, the stubby Lewis tower would serve as little more than an inlet light. Meade felt that the station was strategically located and deserved a more powerful light, with a range sufficient to guide ships at sea. He concluded that the board had little choice but to replace the collapsing structure with a much taller and better-built tower.

Meade's point of view got plenty of support from mariners. Almost from the moment it went into service in 1835, captains complained about the weakness of the light. Some said it was often "impossible to tell whether it is a ship's light or a lighthouse." Mail steamer Captain H. K. Davenport described the light as "indifferent."

Acting on Meade's advice, the board erected a soaring tower, its lantern room perched 163 feet above the inlet. Fitted with a first-order Fresnel lens, the tower exhibited its powerful new light for the first time on January 1, 1859, and the station entered a new era as a true seacoast light. The nation was about to enter a new era as well. Only a few years after his visit to Barnegat in 1855, lighthouse inspector Meade would serve his country in a very different and significant way. As General Meade, he commanded the Army of the Potomac during the last years of the Civil War.

## HOW TO GET THERE:

Take Route 72 to Long Beach Island and follow the signs to Barnegat Lighthouse State Park. Along the way you'll pass through Surf City, North Beach, Harvey Cedars, and Loveladies. The lighthouse is open daily, Memorial Day to Labor Day, and weekends only in May, September, and October. Visitors may take a self-guided tour to the top of the light.

# ABSECON LIGHT

*Atlantic City, New Jersey – 1857*

Nowadays vacationers who travel to Atlantic City to enjoy its sparkling oceanside resorts may be mesmerized by the flashing lights of the big casinos. But for much of its early history, this stretch of the Atlantic shoreline was mostly dark at night. Despite the threat of shoals and shallows lurking just offshore, there was no lighthouse to warn ships of the danger.

Dr. Jonathan Pitney, looked upon by many as the founder of Atlantic City, fought a lifelong battle with federal authorities to have a lighthouse constructed at this site.

Unfortunately for Dr. Pitney, his efforts ran aground on the stubbornness of Fifth Auditor Stephen Pleasonton, the tightfisted Treasury Department bureaucrat who presided over the U.S. Lighthouse Service as if it were his own medieval fiefdom. Pitney confronted Pleasonton with stacks of reports detailing New Jersey shore shipwrecks going all the way back to the 1700s. Despite the evidence, the fifth auditor maintained that there was no money for a midcoast New Jersey lighthouse—and scant need of one.

It was only after Pleasonton lost his grip on the service when Congress created the Lighthouse Board during the early 1850s that the Abescon project finally got under way. It would be one of three New Jersey lighthouses built at about that time, the others being Barnegat and Cape May. All three of these impressive structures are slender towers in excess of 170 feet tall.

The area around what is now Atlantic City was orginally called Absegame after the Indian tribe that once lived in this area. For the new lighthouse to be built here, officials selected a slightly corrupted version of the same name: Absecon. In August 1854 Congress appropriated $35,000 for the Absecon project, and work was soon begun.

It was slow going, however; water from a nearby salt marsh kept filling the foundation pit. Crews tried bucket brigades and manned hand pumps, but to no avail. Eventually, a newfangled steam pump was successfully applied to the task, and workers were able to pour the foundation. Then the money ran out. Only after Congress coughed up an additional $17,000 could work be completed.

Supervising the last stages of construction was Major George G. Meade, a little-known U.S. Army engineer. Only a few years later, he would be better known as General Meade, commander of the Union Army of the Potomac. In 1863 Meade managed another carefully engineered undertaking—the Union victory at Gettysburg.

Fitted with a state-of-the-art, first-order Fresnel lens, the Absecon Lighthouse was at long last ready for service by early 1857, and keeper Daniel Scull first lit its whale-oil lamps on January 15 of that year. The light would burn each night, more or less without interruption, for more than sixty-five years.

Its career, however, could have been much shorter. During the 1870s the ocean threatened to destroy the tower by cutting away its foundation. The tower had been built a quarter of a mile from the nearest ocean waves, but by 1876 storm-driven erosion had brought the Atlantic within two dozen yards of the foundation.

Engineers put forward several plans for saving the lighthouse. One of the least probable of these called for lifting the enormous tower onto rails and moving it a mile inland—all for only $10,000 and supposedly without missing a single night of service. Officials chose a simpler and more likely solution, that of building a long jetty to block the path of the eroding sand. So successful was the jetty, completed in 1878, that, within two years, the ocean had pulled back more than 1,300 feet to its original distance from the lighthouse.

Although the Absecon Lighthouse won its tug-of-war with the ocean, it eventually succumbed to progress. By the early twentieth century, what had once been a lonely coastal village had grown into a bustling city. Buildings obscured the beacon, and mariners could not distinguish it from the bright lights of Atlantic City. In 1933 the Coast Guard discontinued the light and deeded the tower to the city. It still stands today, among the tallest of Atlantic City's many brightly lit attractions.

## HOW TO GET THERE:

Located at the intersection of Vermont and Pacific avenues in Atlantic City, the Absecon Lighthouse was handsomely restored during the 1960s. During the last decade, however, it has fallen on hard times. A more recent, state-funded project aims to restore the old lighthouse to its former glory.

# HEREFORD INLET LIGHT

*North Wildwood, New Jersey – 1874*

A lovely structure of considerable architectural interest, the Hereford Inlet Lighthouse was built in 1873–74 by the Army Corps of Engineers. A stick-style frame building, with a long porch, delicate balusters, and a four-story square tower pushing up through the center of a pitched roof, its fanciful appearance strongly suggests the Victorian era that produced it. Oddly enough, this seemingly unique structure has a near twin, the Point Fermin Lighthouse, built at about the same time in Southern California.

Completed at a relatively modest cost of $25,000, this unusual lighthouse was nonetheless a sturdy piece of work. Lieutenant Colonel W. F. Reynolds, the army engineer who had also supervised construction of the massive Barnegat tower farther to the north, made sure that the Hereford Inlet Lighthouse had the solid construction necessary to stand up to Atlantic storms.

In 1889 a hurricane crashed into the coast of southern New Jersey, drowning many coastal residents and driving thousands from their homes. Among those who counted themselves lucky were eighteen people who took refuge in the Hereford Inlet Lighthouse. The building was soon surrounded by turbulent waters. Although shaken by high wind and pounded by waves, the lighthouse and its frightened guests survived.

Despite storms and a couple of nearly disastrous fires, the Hereford Inlet Lighthouse remained in service for ninety years. Discontinued by the Coast Guard in 1964, it was replaced by a far less attractive, skeleton-type tower. The grounds were transferred to the State of New Jersey and the building boarded up to thwart vandals. So it sat until 1986, when the citizens of North Wildwood successfully petitioned the Coast Guard and received permission to reopen the lighthouse and operate it privately as an aid to navigation.

## HOW TO GET THERE:

Near the far south end of the Garden State Parkway, take the Route 147 exit and drive east toward the Atlantic into North Wildwood. The lighthouse stands just off Central Avenue, between Chestnut and First streets, and is open during the summer. Hours vary.

*The Hereford Inlet Lighthouse is open to the public during the summer, but hours vary. Though quite distinctive, this stick-style Victorian has a near twin: Point Fermin Light in Los Angeles, California.*

# CAPE MAY LIGHT

*Cape May Point, New Jersey – 1824, 1847, and 1859*

At 157 ½ feet tall, the tower of the Cape May Lighthouse soars above the flat, sandy New Jersey coastline and the blue Atlantic beyond. Built in 1859, the distinctive white tower still guides shipping along the coast and into Delaware Bay. The enormous tower replaced two earlier structures dating to 1824 and 1847, respectively.

Exactly 199 steps lead from the ground floor to the lantern room. The focal plane of the extraordinary 600,000-candlepower beacon is 165 feet above sea level.

While the lighthouse is still active, it has been automated; most of the outbuildings and the keepers' dwellings are no longer in use. The keepers' houses are currently under restoration.

According to local tradition (and to rangers at Cape May Point State Park), the old lighthouse has a certain strong influence on young lovers. More than one proposal of marriage has been made—and accepted—atop the tower.

## HOW TO GET THERE:

Follow the Garden State Parkway south until it ends at Cape May. Take Route 109 south and then Lafayette Street almost to the Atlantic. Then turn right onto Sunset Boulevard and follow it to Lighthouse Avenue. Turn right and enter Cape May Point State Park. There is a small admission fee to the lighthouse. For current park hours and fees, call (609) 884–5404.

*The grand white tower of Cape May Lighthouse soars 157½ feet into the New Jersey skies. Built in 1859, the tall lighthouse has guided ships into Delaware Bay since before the Civil War. A smaller tower was built here in 1824. (© William Kaufhold)*

# CHAPTER THREE

# Lights of
# THE BIG BAYS
### DELAWARE and MARYLAND

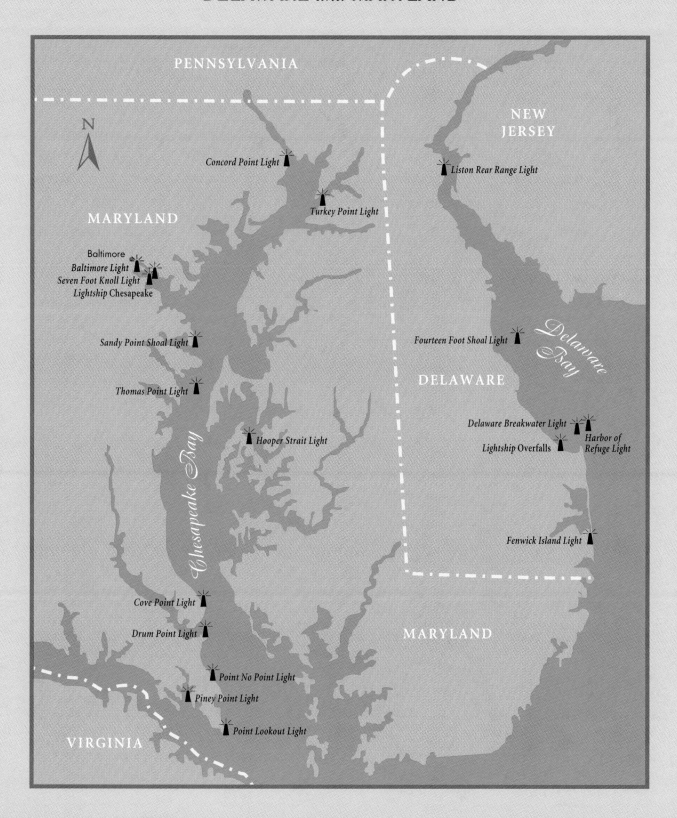

PENNSYLVANIA

NEW
JERSEY

N

Concord Point Light

Liston Rear Range Light

MARYLAND

Turkey Point Light

Baltimore
Baltimore Light
Seven Foot Knoll Light
Lightship Chesapeake

Sandy Point Shoal Light

Fourteen Foot Shoal Light

*Delaware Bay*

DELAWARE

Thomas Point Light

*Chesapeake Bay*

Hooper Strait Light

Delaware Breakwater Light

Harbor of
Refuge Light

Lightship Overfalls

Fenwick Island Light

Cove Point Light

Drum Point Light

MARYLAND

Point No Point Light

Piney Point Light

Point Lookout Light

VIRGINIA

*The octagonal, cottage-style Thomas Point Lighthouse presides over a chilly winter's morning on the Chesapeake Bay.* (© Mark Riddick/New Light Photography)

uch like the ships and sailors who depend on them, lighthouses are perishable. Many of the nation's earliest lighthouses disappeared long ago. Storms bowled them over, or floods and beach erosion cut away their foundations, causing them to topple into the sea. A few were cut down by cannonballs, explosives, and other weapons of war. A surprising number fell victim to the same people who had them built in the first place—members of the Lighthouse Service or Coast Guard who pulled them down to make way for newer, supposedly better navigational facilities. Many others simply grew old and fell down from neglect.

Whenever a lighthouse is destroyed, America loses part of its heritage, a reminder of the often-heroic struggles of the past. But not all vanished lighthouses are lost forever. Indeed, some are eventually rebuilt by the government or by local societies for use as museums. Others continue to be celebrated in books, songs, and memory. In a few instances, lights that no longer shine are still shown on navigation charts. Some old salts swear that, when the weather is just right, they can see a ghostly light emanating from a point where a demolished lighthouse once stood.

Some fallen lighthouses played too important in the nation's history ever to be forgotten. One such was the Cape Henlopen Lighthouse in Delaware.

## SAGA *of the* CAPE HENLOPEN LIGHT

The Cape Henlopen Lighthouse was the seventh major light tower built in the original thirteen American colonies. Completed in 1765, it was financed and operated not by the people of Delaware but by those of Pennsylvania. The merchants of Philadelphia made handsome profits on goods brought by ships moving up the Delaware River. Naturally, they wanted to make the trip to their bustling wharves as easy and safe as possible.

In a manner that might seem familiar to citizens nowadays, Pennsylvania officials attempted to raise money for the project by means of a lottery. Proceeds of the game fell considerably short of the 7,674 pounds sterling needed for construction, however, so the provincial assembly issued a series of lighthouse bonds, at six-percent interest, to make up the difference.

Built at considerably more expense than most other eighteenth-century American lighthouses, the Cape Henlopen tower was made to last. Construction crews used granite brought from quarries upriver near Wilmington, Delaware. Laying the granite down in courses, they gave the tower fortresslike walls, six feet thick at the base and sixty-nine feet tall. It had eight interior levels, each with its own window. On the eighth level was the lantern room, glassed in on all sides. A wooden stairway wound around the inner walls of the tower, providing access to the top. The original lamps were fueled by whale oil when it was available and by lard oil at other times. The tower stood on a sandy hill, which boosted the light to a level more then 115 feet above the water. Some captains claimed to have seen it from seventeen miles at sea.

Pointing the way to prosperous Philadelphia, the Cape Henlopen Lighthouse quickly became one of the most important landmarks in North America. Thousands of British and colonial ships followed its guidance and noted the light in their logs.

It had shone for only a few years, however, when relations between the colonists and their mother country began to sour. By 1775 hostilities seemed inevitable, and the colonists placed a lookout in the Cape Henlopen tower to watch for approaching warships. Should he spot an invasion fleet, the lookout's duty was to ride for Philadelphia hell-for-leather, Paul Revere style, to give the warning.

Instead of an invading armada, the British sent individual warships to harass the colonists. The colonials fought back with a tiny fleet of their own. The young John Paul Jones served aboard one of these

## LISTON REAR RANGE LIGHT

*Port Penn, Delaware – 1877 and 1906*

Range lighthouses operate in pairs to mark channels for shipping. Arrayed one behind the other with the rear light on a higher plane, the beacons will be seen in perfect vertical alignment by the pilots of ships sailing safely through the channel. But if the upper light appears to tilt either to the left or right of vertical, the vessel is straying out of the channel in the direction indicated, and a course correction must be made.

Over the years several range lighthouses have served ships moving up through the Delaware Bay toward the bustling port cities of Wilmington and Philadelphia. Perhaps the most remarkable of these is the Liston Rear Range Lighthouse, located near Port Penn, Delaware. Most range lighthouse towers are of relatively modest height, but this one is 120 feet tall, and its light has a focal plane more than 175 feet above the waters of the bay. A black metal cylinder supported by a pyramid-shaped steel skeleton, it was built in 1877. Originally, its lofty lantern room held a second-order Fresnel lens. Although the Fresnel was removed when the station was automated in 1976, the airport-style beacon that replaced it can boast five-million candlepower. Located some distance away and closer to the river, the front range tower is forty-five feet tall and dates from 1906. Both lights remain in operation.

### HOW TO GET THERE:

Take U.S. Highway 13 north from Dover or south from Wilmington and turn eastward onto Road 2. The Liston light station is located less than a mile from Highway 13.

*The Liston Rear Range Lighthouse, near Port Penn, is one of a pair of lights marking the safe channel through Delaware Bay. (© Mark Riddick/ New Light Photography)*

The Fourteen Foot Shoal Lighthouse marks an important navigational obstacle in Delaware Bay just off Bowers Beach. The cast-iron tower and dwelling rest on a concrete caisson completely surrounded by the waters of the bay. The existing structure dates from 1888. It replaced an earlier tower built in 1776. The station employs a fourth-order Fresnel lens with a focal plane fifty-nine feet above the water. (Courtesy U.S. Coast Guard)

The lightship Overfalls *spent most of its operational life in New England. Launched at a Maine shipyard in 1938, it served at the important Boston station and several other locations off Massachusetts and Connecticut. It guided ships with a light fixed atop a central mast. With a length of 116 feet and a beam of 25 feet, the diesel-powered* Overfalls *is typical of vessels in the now-retired Coast Guard lightship fleet. The Lewes County Historical Society acquired the lightship shortly after it was decommissioned in 1973. Berthed off Mulberry Street in Lewes, it now serves as a museum. (Courtesy U.S. Coast Guard)*

# LIGHTHOUSES OF THE HARBOR OF REFUGE

*Delaware Breakwater Light – 1885 and 1926*

*Harbor of Refuge Light – 1896 and 1926*

ales, hurricanes, and nor'easters often rip into America's Mid-Atlantic coast, sometimes striking with little or no warning. Vessels caught in a storm along these shores seek any shelter they can find, but safe harbors that can be reached easily from open water are few and far between. That is why, when violent weather approaches, ships often make a run for the mouth of the Delaware River. There they can hope to ride out the fury of a storm in the relatively quiet waters behind the protective barrier of Cape Henlopen.

Recognizing the importance of this area to shipping, the federal government established, during the late nineteenth century, an anchorage just west of Cape Henlopen. Designating it a "National Harbor of Refuge," the government constructed a series of breakwaters to increase the protection offered by the cape. Two of these were marked by lighthouses.

Completed in 1885, the Delaware Breakwater Lighthouse was positioned so that its light could be seen from both the harbor and ocean. A second lighthouse, built in

*The setting sun seems to explode from the lantern of the Delaware Breakwater Lighthouse.* (© Mark Riddick / New Light Photography)

1896, marked the entrance to the Harbor of Refuge. The two breakwater lights served in conjunction with the much stronger beacon of the nearby Cape Henlopen Lighthouse (see pages 49–51). Fitted with an enormous, first-order Fresnel lens, the Cape Henlopen Lighthouse was one of the best-known and most powerful navigational lights in America. Its days were numbered, however; tottering on a foundation seriously weakened by erosion, the 160-year-old Cape Henlopen tower collapsed in April 1926. Instead of rebuilding the old Cape Henlopen tower, lighthouse officials decided to rely on the existing breakwater lights.

The Delaware Breakwater Light stands on a concrete-and-stone caisson. To help it stand up to storms, the forty-nine-foot brick tower is encased in iron plates. The lantern room once held a fourth-order Fresnel lens, but this was replaced by an airport-style beacon when the station was automated in 1973.

Damaged by a series of storms, the thirty-year-old tower marking the harbor entrance was abandoned in 1926. It was replaced by the Harbor of Refuge Breakwater Lighthouse, built that same year. Located in a caisson at the south end of the outer-harbor breakwater, its cast-iron tower stands seventy-six feet tall. Originally fitted with a fourth-order Fresnel lens, it was automated in 1973 and given an optic similar to that of its neighbor across the harbor. Both of these breakwater lights remain in operation, serving storm-battered ships in search of a safe harbor.

## HOW TO GET THERE:

From U.S. Highway 9 follow Route 18 to Cape Henlopen State Park. The lighthouses can be seen from several points along the main park road. The beaches here are extremely pleasant, and there are plenty of good spots for picnicking.

*Exposed to the often violent Atlantic, the Harbor of Refuge Lighthouse stands secure atop a massive concrete caisson.* (© Mark Riddick/New Light Photography)

# FENWICK ISLAND LIGHT

*Fenwick Island, Delaware – 1858*

Fenwick Island Light is actually in Delaware, which was once part of Pennsylvania, but it can be viewed without ever leaving Maryland because the transpeninsular line, an early survey that became part of the Mason–Dixon line, ran through the lighthouse property, separating Delaware and Maryland. In fact, Mr. Mason and Mr. Dixon began their famous survey on Fenwick Island and used the transpeninsular marker, which had been placed years earlier, in 1750, as the start of their famous line between the North and the South.

Built in 1858 to guide ships into Delaware Bay, Fenwick Island Lighthouse is eighty-seven feet tall, with a focal plane of eighty-three feet above sea level. It holds a third-order Fresnel lens. The first painting of the lighthouse cost the United States government exactly $5.00.

The lighthouse is owned by the State of Delaware and is maintained by the nonprofit Friends of Fenwick Island. The lighthouse is open to the public and depends upon private contributions for most of its maintenance. The light, visible from fifteen miles at sea, fills an otherwise dark gap between Assateague Light in Virginia and the Cape Henlopen Light to the north.

## HOW TO GET THERE:

Fenwick Island Lighthouse is located 2 blocks west of Route 1 on 146th Street in North Ocean City, Maryland. The tower is open Memorial Day through Labor Day and at other times by appointment. For more information contact Paul Pepper, president and founder of the Friends of Fenwick Island Lighthouse, at P.O. Box 6, Selbyville, DE 19975; (410) 250–1098.

*The Fenwick Island Light stands just north of the Mason–Dixon Line, which runs right past the tower. Although the lighthouse receives some financial support from the state of Delaware, it is maintained by volunteers. Interested people are encouraged to join the Friends of Fenwick Island, a nonprofit organization.*

# TURKEY POINT LIGHT

*Elk Neck, Maryland – 1833*

Turkey Point juts southward into the Chesapeake Bay near its far north end. A modest masonry light tower has stood here since 1833, its beacon guiding ships headed for the Susquehanna River. Although the tower is only thirty-eight feet tall, it stands on a hundred-foot-high bluff, which gives it a considerable boost in height and effectiveness.

The government paid contractor John Donohoo $4,355 to build the tower and nearby keeper's dwelling. Donohoo built a number of Chesapeake lighthouses, including those at Thomas Point, Piney Point, and Point Lookout.

For more than twenty years, the Turkey Point Lighthouse was home to Mrs. Harry Salter, the last female in the nation's corps of civilian keepers. She had received her appointment from President Calvin Coolidge in 1925 after the death of her husband, the previous keeper. Mrs. Salter retired when the station was automated in 1947. Earlier female keepers had served here as well, including Elizabeth Lusby, who kept the light burning from 1844 to 1861, and Clara Blumfield, who held the keeper's post from 1895 to 1919.

## HOW TO GET THERE:

Only the lighthouse tower still stands. It is located at the far end of pristine Elk Neck State Park, a major game preserve. The park and lighthouse are accessible to the public via Route 272. Follow I–95 north from Baltimore and look for the Route 272 exit several miles past the Susquehanna Bridge. When approaching from Wilmington, Delaware, the Route 272 exit is about 12 miles beyond the Maryland state line.

*The Turkey Point Light has marked the far northern end of Chesapeake Bay since 1833.*
(© Mark Riddick/New Light Photography)

# CONCORD POINT LIGHT

*Havre de Grace, Maryland – 1827*

Two years after he had built the Thomas Point Lighthouse—and botched the job—John Donohoo won a contract to erect a lighthouse on Concord Point at Havre de Grace. Donohoo completed the thirty-two-foot stone tower in less than a year for $3,500, and this time his work was solid. The tower still stands today, looking very much as it did when its lamps were first lit in 1827.

Originally, the lantern held a set of lamps and sixteen-inch reflectors. Later these were exchanged for a fifth-order Fresnel lens, among the smallest Fresnels available. Today the tower displays a fixed white light as a private aid to navigation. It has been automated since the 1920s.

All the keepers of the Concord Point Light came from a single family, that of war hero John O'Niel. During the War of 1812, O'Niel had made a quixotic one-man stand against an entire British fleet. Miraculously, he survived and later was rewarded with the post of keeper at the Concord Point Light. The job was passed down from one generation of O'Niels to the next. Finally, in the 1920s, the light was automated, and great-grandson Harry O'Niel had to surrender the tower key.

## HOW TO GET THERE:

Take State 155 off I–95 into Havre de Grace and turn left onto Otsego Street. Then turn right onto Saint John's Street and, finally, left again at the sign for Concord Point. If you get lost, remember that the light is near the Susquehanna River in the southeast part of town.

*The lighthouse is open for tours every Saturday and Sunday from 1:00 P.M. to 5:00 P.M. from April through October. For more information contact the Friends of Concord Point Lighthouse, Box 212, Havre de Grace, MD 21078; (410) 939–3303.*

*The thirty-two-foot stone tower on Concord Point was completed at a cost of $3,500—in 1827.*

# THOMAS POINT LIGHT

*Chesapeake Bay, Maryland – 1825, 1838, and 1875*

The growth of shipping on the Chesapeake convinced the government to build a small tower on Thomas Point, not far from Annapolis. A bank of treacherous shoals extending out into the Chesapeake forced vessels requiring deep water to swing wide around the point. Obviously, a light was needed to help them keep their distance at night. In 1824 federal officials bought seven acres on the point for about $500 and hired a novice contractor named John Donohoo to construct a small tower for about $5,600. The inexperienced Donohoo did a poor job of building the tower, however, and a few years later, it had to be torn down and rebuilt.

The contract for reconstruction of the Thomas Point Lighthouse went to Winslow Lewis, who held a patent on the "reflecting and magnifying" lantern used in many American lighthouses (Lewis's system was eventually shown to be inadequate and was replaced in most lighthouses by high-quality Fresnel lenses). Lewis rebuilt the lighthouse for only about $2,500, and his tower guarded the point for more than thirty years. But its light was weak, and Chesapeake sailors grumbled that it was "utterly useless" in fog or foul weather.

In 1875 the Lighthouse Board decided to move the light offshore and place it where it would be most effective—out in the bay, immediately over the shoals. The new lighthouse was a small, hexagon-shaped building perched on screw piles. Abandoned, the Lewis tower on the point eventually collapsed, but for more than a century, the light on the shoals has weathered storms, floods, and ice floes—everything that nature has thrown at it. The Thomas Point Light remains active.

## HOW TO GET THERE:

The only way to see this lighthouse is by boat. Annapolis, Maryland, is the nearest port. For possible sightseeing boat tours, contact the Tourism Council of Annapolis and Anne Arundel County, One Annapolis Street, Annapolis, MD 21401; (301) 280–0445.

*The Thomas Point Light remains on the shoals of Chesapeake Bay, where it has stood since 1875.* (© Mark Riddick / New Light Photography)

# SEVEN FOOT KNOLL LIGHT

*Baltimore, Maryland – 1855*

On August 21, 1933, Maryland was hit by a storm so violent that it destroyed hundreds of homes and boats along the Atlantic coast and in the Chesapeake Bay. Out on the bay, the dark-red, cheese-box-shaped Seven Foot Knoll Lighthouse was torn by ninety-mile-per-hour winds and pounded by fifteen-foot waves. The lighthouse trembled and shook, but keeper Thomas Steinise was sure it would stand up to the beating, just as it had so many times in the past.

Then, above the roar of the wind, he heard a disturbing sound—the high-pitched signal of a vessel in distress. The call came from *Point Breeze,* a tugboat that had been running for the safety of some protective harbor when it was caught and overwhelmed by the waves.

The hapless tug sank within 500 yards of the lighthouse. Facing near-certain death, Steinise lowered the station's twenty-one-foot dory into the chaotic waters and pulled with all his strength for the wreck. For more than two hours, the keeper battled the storm single-handedly in his open boat. He managed to rescue the six crewmen.

For his part in the dramatic rescue, Steinise was awarded the Congressional Medal for heroism. "Just doing what was right," the modest Steinise told reporters.

Seven Foot Knoll is the oldest surviving example of the Chesapeake's classic screw-pile lighthouses. Completed in 1855, it served mariners as an active light or daymark for more than 130 years. Designed for a third-order lens, it received a fourth-order Fresnel instead. During fog and heavy weather, the keeper sounded a bell.

First automated and then put out of service by the Coast Guard, the lighthouse was eventually donated to the City of Baltimore for use as a museum. In 1988 the 220-ton structure was cut from its pilings and carried on a barge to its current location at Pier 5, in the city's popular Inner Harbor district.

*Shown here on a permanent display in Baltimore, the bright red Seven Foot Knoll Lighthouse once marked the entrance to the city's heavily trafficked harbor.*

## HOW TO GET THERE:

From I–95 take the Pratt Street exit and follow the signs to the Baltimore Inner Harbor. There are several parking lots in the area just off Pratt Street. The lighthouse is located near the end of Pier 5. For hours and other information, call (410) 685–0295. While at the Inner Harbor, be sure to visit the nearby lightship Chesapeake. The Baltimore Inner Harbor offers several excellent restaurants and plenty of intriguing shops. For those interested in undersea life, the National Aquarium, located near Pier 5, is a must-see.

# LIGHTSHIP *CHESAPEAKE*

*Baltimore, Maryland – 1930*

With an overall length of 133 feet, a thirty-foot beam, and a displacement of only 130 gross tons, the *Chesapeake* is a feisty little vessel. Launched in 1930, she guided ships in and out of Chesapeake Bay until World War II, when German U-boats menaced shipping along the Eastern Seaboard. Fitted with a pair of twenty-mm guns, the *Chesapeake* was drafted into the Navy and served out the war as a harbor-patrol boat. Following the war she became a lightship once again and returned to her original duty station.

Decommissioned by the Coast Guard in 1971, the hard-working *Chesapeake* became a seagoing environmental classroom for schoolchildren. Since 1988, when it was loaned to the City of Baltimore, the ship has provided a different sort of education. As one of the most popular exhibits at the Baltimore Maritime Museum, it reminds visitors of the historic role of lightships in the nation's history.

## HOW TO GET THERE:

From I–95 take the Pratt Street exit and follow the signs to the Baltimore Inner Harbor. There are several parking lots available just off Pratt Street in the Inner Harbor area. The lightship Chesapeake *is berthed in the harbor near the intersection of Pratt and Gay streets. Nearby is the* USS Constellation, *one of the nation's early wooden fighting ships.*

*On station for decades in the Atlantic near the entrance to Chesapeake Bay, the lightship* Chesapeake *later served for a time as an environmental classroom. Today it is a popular exhibit at the Baltimore Maritime Museum.*

# SANDY POINT SHOAL LIGHT

*Skidmore, Maryland – 1883*

With its mansard roof and pitched dormer windows, the Sandy Shoal Lighthouse looks more like an old Victorian residence than a navigational marker. Its location is distinctly maritime, however, as it is located almost a mile offshore and surrounded by the choppy waters of Chesapeake Bay.

A dangerous shoal extends from Maryland's Sandy Point nearly a mile out into the Chesapeake. Countless vessels have come to grief on this obstacle, which is made all the more threatening by a significant narrowing of the bay between Jones Point on the west and Kent Island to the east. In 1858 the Lighthouse Board established a light station onshore at Sandy Point, but it was of only limited use to pilots trying to avoid the shoal, especially in fog or stormy weather.

After petitioning Congress many times to provide funds for a new and better lighthouse, the board finally secured $25,000 for the project in 1882. Completed the following year, the two-and-a-half-story brick structure stands on a thirty-five-foot-wide, concrete-and-stone caisson at the outer edge of the shoal. A combination dwelling-and-tower, it rises fifty feet above the waters of the bay. The fanciful design reflects the Victorian era in which it was built. Automated in 1963, the light remains in operation, displaying a white flash ten times every minute.

## HOW TO GET THERE:

*The Sandy Point Shoal Lighthouse can be reached only by boat and is off-limits to the public. It can be seen to the north as you cross the Chesapeake Bay Bridge; if you are driving, however, please keep your eyes on the road. The best place to view the light is from Sandy Point State Park, accessible from an exit off U.S. Highway 50 just west of the bridge tollbooths. The park is also a great place to have a picnic and enjoy the Chesapeake scenery.*

*Built on a caisson in the middle of Chesapeake Bay, the Sandy Point Shoal Lighthouse can be seen (actually, it is rather hard to miss) from the Maryland end of the well-known Bay Bridge.*

(© Mark Riddick/New Light Photography)

# HOOPER STRAIT LIGHT

*Saint Michaels, Maryland – 1867 and 1879*

For more than forty years, beginning in 1827, the crooked channel of Hooper Strait was marked by a lightship. But in 1867 the Lighthouse Board built a modest screw-pile tower there to guide shipping. Ten years later a massive ice floe swept the little lighthouse off its piles and carried it five miles down the bay. A tender found the wreckage and managed to salvage the lens and some of the equipment.

A larger, hexagonal lighthouse had replaced the crushed tower by the autumn of 1879, and it remained in service for three quarters of a century. Deactivated in 1954, it was eventually acquired by the Chesapeake Bay Maritime Museum in Saint Michaels, on the Maryland eastern shore. In order to move the forty-four-foot-wide structure down the Chesapeake to Saint Michaels, museum officials had it cut in half, like a giant apple, and loaded onto a barge. Reassembled and restored to like-new condition, the lighthouse now stands beside the museum on Navy Point.

## HOW TO GET THERE:

To reach the museum and lighthouse, take U.S. Highway 50 north from Cambridge and then State 33 east to Saint Michaels, a charming Chesapeake Bay community. The museum, which is near the downtown area on Navy Point, is a village in itself, with houses, stores, a restaurant, and wonderful exhibits of small boats used by the bay watermen.

The lighthouse is surrounded by historic workboats and oyster sailboats at nearby docks, giving you the feeling that you have stepped back in time. The Hooper Strait Lighthouse, one of the three remaining screw-pile lighthouses in the Chesapeake Bay, is a cottage-type structure. It was moved to the museum site in 1966 and has been restored and furnished in turn-of-the-century style. Even the white-and-red-checkered tablecloth on the kitchen table looks as if the keeper's mug of hot coffee were about to be set upon it.

For more information write the Chesapeake Bay Maritime Museum, Box 636, Saint Michaels, MD 21663.

# COVE POINT LIGHT

*Solomons, Maryland – 1828*

For the better part of two centuries, mariners navigating the long middle reaches of Chesapeake Bay have watched for the powerful flash of Cove Point Lighthouse. At night the 150,000-candlepower light breaks over the dark waters of the bay every ten seconds. The Cove Point beacon is so bright, in fact, that it sometimes disturbs the sleep of nearby residents.

Years ago a neighbor complained bitterly that the flashing light made it, not just difficult, but impossible for her to get any rest. Several times a minute, all night long, it blasted through her bedroom window, turning night into day. Apparently a lady of some influence, she demanded that something be done. To help her rest in peace, keepers hung an opaque curtain in the section of the lantern facing her house. As a result the Coast Guard *Light List* notes that the beacon is obscured from 040 to 110 degrees. Navigators who suddenly and mysteriously lose sight of the light on a dark Chesapeake night might find the explanation interesting.

Among the oldest lighthouses on the Chesapeake, Cove Point marks the entrance to the Patuxent River. The conical, fifty-one-foot brick tower is the work of John Donohoo, a contractor from Havre de Grace. Donohoo also built the original Thomas Point tower and several other early Chesapeake lighthouses. The Cove Point Lighthouse was among his best, for it has stood intact since 1828.

Erosion threatened the structure almost from the day it was completed. By the 1840s keepers were reporting severe shore erosion, and retaining walls were built to hold back the bay, enabling the tower to survive at least another 150 years. Today the Chesapeake has cut to within a few feet of the old tower and may still claim its victim.

Although the light is now automated, Cove Point remains an active Coast Guard station and is off-limits to visitors. The area is easily accessible from nearby Solomons, Maryland, however, and the lighthouse can be viewed from the station fence.

## HOW TO GET THERE:

Follow Maryland Highway 4 southeast from the Washington, D.C., Beltway to the town of Solomons. Here one can visit the Drum Point Lighthouse before proceeding to Cove Point. From Solomons take Cove Point Road to the Cove Point Coast Guard Station. Best viewing of the light is from about half an hour before sunset until just after dark. Helpful information may be obtained from the Calvert Marine Museum in Solomons at (301) 326–2042.

*Still on active duty, the Cove Point Lighthouse stands watch at a Coast Guard station.* (Courtesy Frank L. Parks)

# DRUM POINT LIGHT

*Solomons, Maryland – 1883*

Many screw-pile lighthouses once stood in the shallow Chesapeake, but today only a few remain. One of these is Drum Point Lighthouse, a hexagonal, cottage-type lighthouse built on ten-inch, wrought-iron piles. Now part of a museum in Solomons, it once marked the north entrance of the Patuxent River.

Erected in 1883, the lighthouse cost $5,000 and took only about a month to build. Fitted with a fourth-order Fresnel lens, it showed a fixed red light, warning vessels of the sandy spit off the point. Having served for almost eight decades, Drum Point Light was taken out of active service in 1962.

## HOW TO GET THERE:

Take Maryland Highway 4 south from Washington, D.C., to Solomons. The museum and lighthouse are on the left just before the bridge over the Patuxent River. The lighthouse has been wonderfully restored and furnished in early 1900s style. There is a small admission fee.

The museum offers exhibits on the paleontology, estuarine biology, and maritime history of the region. For hours and additional information, contact Calvert Marine Museum, Box 97, Solomons, Maryland; (410) 326–2042.

*The Drum Point Lighthouse (bottom), on display at Solomons, Maryland, is one of the Chesapeake's few surviving screw-pile-type towers. The handsome fourth-order Fresnel lens (above) distorts the view.*

# POINT LOOKOUT LIGHT

*St. Mary's City, Maryland – 1830*

Strategically positioned between the Chesapeake Bay on the east and the mouth of the Potomac River on the west, the long, skinny finger of Point Lookout has been marked by a light since 1830. This was never a major light station, however. The $3,350 the Congress provided for the project proved sufficient only for a modest house with a small lantern perched on its roof.

This arrangement placed the light just twenty-four feet above the waters of the bay, and it could be seen from only a few miles away. While it helped ships avoid slamming into the point, it was otherwise of little use to navigators. Later the house was enlarged and the lantern raised to more than forty feet, which considerably improved its range and usefulness.

The Coast Guard deactivated the station in 1966, replacing it with a more effective light on a nearby skeleton tower.

The lighthouse is now part of Point Lookout State Park.

Navigators have often scratched their heads when they examine nautical charts of this part of the Chesapeake Bay. Not far from Point Lookout are Point Looking and Point No Point.

## HOW TO GET THERE:

The lighthouse is located in Point Lookout State Park, at the very end of Maryland Highway 5, a few miles south of St. Mary's City. The park plans to restore the old lighthouse and open it to the public. The park itself is a wonder for anyone who loves water, as it affords a nearly 360-degree view of the blue Chesapeake.

*The remains of a rare lower-Chesapeake snowfall give this view of the Point Lookout Lighthouse a wintry feeling.* (© Mark Riddick/New Light Photography)

# PINEY POINT LIGHT

*Valley Lee, Maryland – 1836*

Several U.S. presidents, including James Madison, used Piney Point as a summer retreat. For this reason, some refer to the old light station here as the "lighthouse of the presidents." President Madison had come and gone for the last time, however, long before the lighthouse was built here in 1836.

A conical masonry cylinder only thirty-five feet tall, the Piney Point tower was built by John Donohoo for approximately $5,000. (Donohoo built many of Maryland's early lighthouses.)

In 1855 the station received a fourth-order Fresnel lens, making it the most prominent light on the Potomac. The light guided shipping traveling between Washington, D.C., and the open waters of the Chesapeake Bay. The light remained in operation for more than one and a quarter centuries before the Coast Guard deactivated it in 1964. The station now serves as a lighthouse museum.

## HOW TO GET THERE:

*The lighthouse is located off Piney Point Road several miles south of Valley Lee, Maryland. To reach Valley Lee follow Maryland Highway 5 to Callaway and turn right onto Route 249. The Piney Point Lighthouse Museum, housed in a separate building near the Piney Point Lighthouse, depicts the story of lighthouses on the Potomac River. For hours and other information, contact the St. Clements Island–Potomac River Museum at (301) 769–2222.*

*The squat Piney Point Lighthouse is sometimes known as the "lighthouse of the presidents."* (© Mark Riddick/New Light Photography)

# CHAPTER FOUR

# *Lights of*
# THE OLD DOMINION
## VIRGINIA

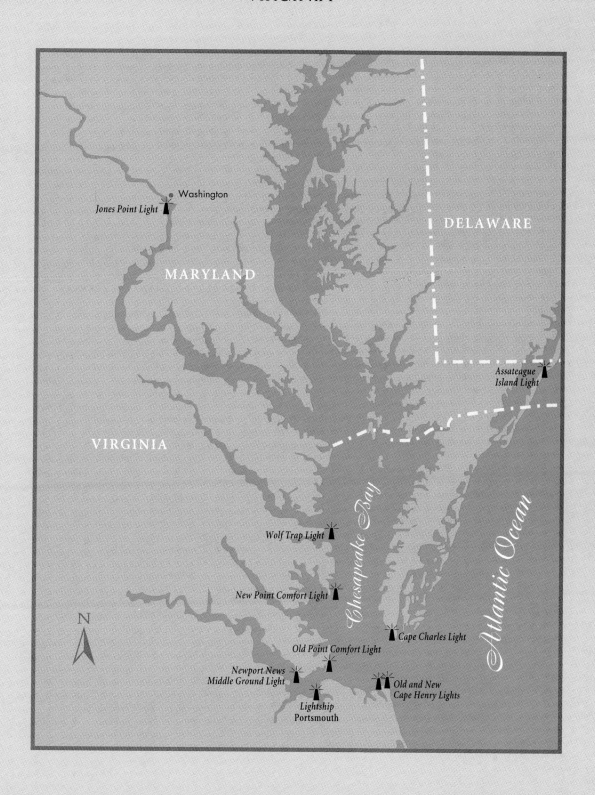

Jones Point Light ● Washington

DELAWARE

MARYLAND

Assateague
Island Light

VIRGINIA

*Chesapeake Bay*

*Atlantic Ocean*

Wolf Trap Light

New Point Comfort Light

N

Cape Charles Light

Old Point Comfort Light

Newport News
Middle Ground Light

Old and New
Cape Henry Lights

Lightship
Portsmouth

W olf Trap Lighthouse, so named because HMS Wolfe was stranded on the shoal here in 1691, is built on a heavy caisson. The light atop the fifty-two-foot tower still flashes its warning every fifteen seconds. An earlier screwpile-type lighthouse, built here in 1870, was swept away by a huge ice floe in 1893. A tender found the structure floating some twenty miles away. (Courtesy Frank L. Parks)

oughly a dozen years after the Revolutionary War siege at Yorktown, the United States government built a lighthouse on Cape Henry, the very place where old Governor Spotswood of colonial Virginia had envisioned a tower and light a lifetime earlier (see page 3). Its fish-oil lamps were first lit one night in October 1792 and were still burning brightly some twenty years later, when British warships returned to the Chesapeake to fight the War of 1812. This time the Royal Navy met far less opposition at the capes than it had in 1781. In fact, the British captains may very well have used the Cape Henry beacon to help them steer their ships into the bay.

The invaders remained in the Chesapeake for more than a year, slamming the door on commerce and terrorizing the population. As the British burned and blasted one bayside community after another, the Americans fought back bravely but ineffectively with a pitiful array of clumsy barges on which they had mounted field cannon. At Hampton Roads the British captured Fort Monroe, using as a watchtower the Old Point Comfort Lighthouse, which had been in service for only about a dozen years.

Eventually, the redcoats attacked the City of Washington itself, setting fire to the Capitol and the White House. At Baltimore the British tried an unsuccessful military experiment, bombing Fort McHenry with rockets launched from small boats in the harbor. Most of the rockets exploded high in the air before they ever reached the fort. The British failed to capture the fort, but the sight of the rockets exploding like fireworks over Fort McHenry inspired Francis Scott Key to write a poem: "Oh say, can you see . . ."

## IRON CLASHES *with* IRON

Almost a half a century after Key penned his famous lines, war again swept over the Chesapeake. This time it was a great Civil War, with American fighting American, North against South. Vastly inferior to the Northern side in naval strength, the Southerners were no friends of lighthouses. To make navigation as difficult as possible for Union sailors, the Confederates snuffed out all but a handful of the lights from Virginia all the way to the Mexican border. The Cape Henry Light was extinguished in 1861, the first year of the struggle. It remained dark in 1862, when the Confederates made their boldest attempt to punch a hole in the tight Union naval blockade of the Southern coasts.

On the morning of March 8, 1862, the Confederate States ship *Virginia* steamed out of the James River and bore down on a squadron of Union frigates anchored in the Chesapeake, within sight of the Old Point Comfort Lighthouse at Fort Monroe. Encased in a shell of iron plates two inches thick, the *Virginia* was a fighting ship such as the world had never seen.

Until this strange vessel appeared from around a bend in the James, sailors on the Union frigate *Cumberland* had been doing laundry and hanging their wet uniforms in the rigging to dry in the breeze. They had reason to be relaxed; as far as they knew, the South had no real navy. The last thing they expected was an attack, but incredibly, an attack was coming. There, in plain sight, was the *Virginia,* lumbering along at its sluggish top speed of five knots directly toward the *Cumberland.*

The laundry was snatched down out of the rigging, and the crew quickly readied the frigate's guns. The *Cumberland* started firing while the *Virginia* was still three-quarters of a mile away. But to their horror, the gunners on the doomed frigate saw their shots bounce harmlessly off the *Virginia*'s thick armor. They reloaded and fired, reloaded and fired, but there was no stopping the *Virginia*. It kept plowing forward until, with a tremendous shock, it drove a 1,500-pound iron ram into the wooden ribs of the *Cumberland*. Mortally wounded, the Union ship went down swiftly, taking much of her crew with her.

That same day, the *Virginia* also destroyed the frigate *Congress* and drove several other Union vessels aground on the spreading Chesapeake mudflats. Then, with night approaching, the Southerners took their seemingly invincible ship back to the James. But on the following day, they brought the *Virginia* out again, meaning to put an end to the Union blockade once and for all. This time, however, there was a surprise waiting for the Confederates. Directly in the path of the *Virginia* lay a low, turreted vessel described by one astonished Southern sailor as a "cheese box on a raft." But this small ship, its deck continuously washed over by the waves, was no joke. It was, in fact, an ironclad like the *Virginia,* part of a whole new class of fighting ships called "monitors."

The *Virginia* and the *Monitor* pounded away at one another for hours, but to little effect. Their historic confrontation ended in a draw. Neither would ever be defeated in battle, though within a few months, both would be sunk. The *Virginia* was scuttled by its own crew to keep it from falling into the hands of Union troops who had overrun the Confederate naval yard at Norfolk. The *Monitor* sank in a fierce storm only a few miles south of the Hatteras Lighthouse.

## U-BOATS *off the* CAPES

The Civil War clash of the ironclads was not the last time that ships would fight near the Virginia capes. Many times between 1942 and 1945, the keepers of the Cape Henry Lighthouse saw flashes in the night and heard the thunder of exploding torpedoes fired by German submarines. Despite heavy patrolling by the Coast Guard and U.S. Navy destroyers, U-boat "wolf packs" often lurked in the waters beyond the capes.

The wolves were especially hungry during the winter and spring of 1942. On January 30 of that year, the tanker *Rochester* received a torpedo amidships and sank within sight of the Cape Henry Light. Two weeks later a pair of torpedoes took down the tanker *E.H. Blum,* also near Cape Henry. On March 20 a German submarine sank the tanker *Oakmar.* In April the tankers *David Atwater* and *Tiger* and the freighters *Robin Hood* and *Alcoa Skipper* were all sent to the bottom by U-boats.

The carnage continued at intervals throughout World War II. The Cape Henry keepers would see a flash or hear a rumble and know that yet another vessel had fallen prey to the unseen enemy beneath the waves. There was little that the keepers could do but watch, lend lifesaving assistance if they could, and keep their lights burning.

*Old Cape Henry Lighthouse still stands after more than two centuries. Built in 1792, its duties were eventually taken over by a second tower completed in 1881.*

# ASSATEAGUE ISLAND LIGHT

*Assateague Island, Virginia – 1833 and 1867*

In 1831 Congress appropriated money for a lighthouse to be built a few miles south of the Maryland border on Assateague Island, about halfway between the Chesapeake and Delaware bays. Its chief duty was to warn ships away from the dangerous shoals that extend from the Maryland and Virginia coasts like knife blades; however, after the light was completed and its lamps lit in January 1833, it proved too weak to perform this task effectively. But nothing was done about the problem for almost a quarter of a century.

Then, during the late 1850s, the Lighthouse Board launched a determined campaign aimed at repairing, upgrading, and correcting the many deficiencies of lighthouses all along the Southern coasts. As part of this comprehensive effort, the board decided to rebuild the Assateague Island tower. The Civil War interrupted the work, and the new lighthouse was not ready for service until October 1867. Once its lamps were lit, however, sailors could easily see the improvement. A first-order Fresnel lens made the light visible from nineteen miles at sea.

The Assateague Island Light is now automated. It stands inside the Chincoteague National Wildlife Refuge, not far from the Assateague Island National Seashore.

## HOW TO GET THERE:

To reach the Chincoteague National Wildlife Refuge from U.S. Highway 13 (the main road down the eastern shore of Virginia), take Virginia Highway 175 to Chincoteague; then follow signs to the refuge across the bridge to Assateague Island. Depending on the season, there may be a small admission fee to enter the wildlife area, which allows hunting. Call (804) 336–6122 for specific information.

Although you can see the lighthouse as you cross the bridge to the island, the tower gets lost behind the trees when you reach the island. The person at the tollbooth can provide directions to the tower. A mile or so beyond the tollbooth is a large parking lot on the right-hand side of the paved road. From the parking lot a trail leads several hundred yards through the woods to the lighthouse.

The tower is painted with red-and-white stripes and looks something like a candy cane without the curving top. A first-order Fresnel lens is on display near the base of the tower. The tower itself is closed to the public because the lighthouse is still in service.

Try going to the lighthouse in the late afternoon. If there are not too many other people in the area, you might see wild deer grazing about the tower as darkness falls.

*The Assateague Island Light has been active since 1833.*

# CAPE CHARLES LIGHT

*Chesapeake Bay, Virginia – 1828, 1864, and 1894*

Some thirty-five years after the Cape Henry Lighthouse began to guide ships into the Chesapeake, a second, smaller tower was built on the opposite lip of the bay. Completed in 1828 at a cost of just under $7,400, the fifty-five-foot Cape Charles Lighthouse did little to improve navigation. Almost from the moment its lamps were lit, skippers complained that the light was hopelessly inadequate. Even under ideal conditions, the light carried only twelve miles; in heavy weather or fog, it could barely be seen at all. Even so, it remained in service for more than three decades before the Lighthouse Board thought of replacing it.

In 1858 the board launched construction of a 150-foot brick tower about a mile from the original Cape Charles Light. But, hampered by storms and shortages of materials, the work moved slowly. At the outbreak of the Civil War, three years after the first brick was laid, the tower had reached only half its intended height. In 1862 a party of Confederate raiders attacked the construction site, driving off the work crew and destroying whatever they could. Another two years were needed to repair the damage and complete the tower. The lamps, which illuminated a first-order Fresnel lens, were finally lit on May 17, 1864.

As with many of the other Southern lights, the nemesis of the Cape Charles Lighthouse has been erosion. In 1883 officials measured the rate of erosion on Cape Charles and discovered with alarm that the sea was moving thirty feet closer to the lighthouse each year.

Workers tried, but failed, to stop the advance with stone jetties. Then an engineering study revealed that halting the erosion would cost $150,000, a truly astounding sum at that time. So the board saw no alternative but to build another tower farther from the encroaching waves.

The new Cape Charles Lighthouse was begun in 1892 and completed two years later on a site roughly a mile inland from the original light station. The 191-foot tower is an iron cylinder only nine feet wide, but it is reinforced by a pyramidal steel superstructure. The lantern is reached by means of a staircase inside the cylinder. Because of its design, unusual for a lighthouse located as far north as Virginia, the tower is strong but relatively light in weight. Since the members of the superstructure offer little resistance to the wind, lighthouses of similar design are often seen along the hurricane-plagued coasts of Florida and the Gulf of Mexico. Now automated, the Cape Charles Light remains in use.

## HOW TO GET THERE:

Even the Coast Guard has trouble getting to this lighthouse. Located on a remote island near the northern lip of the Chesapeake Bay, it is not open to the public.

*The Cape Charles Light's strong but lightweight design is unusual for a lighthouse sited as far north as Virginia.*

# NEW POINT COMFORT LIGHT

*Mathews, Virginia – 1804*

The name *New* Point Comfort at first seems a misnomer, as it is, in fact, one of the oldest major lights in the United States. Built in 1804, it is very nearly the same age as the *Old* Point Comfort Lighthouse, completed in 1802 and located at Fort Monroe, about two dozen miles to the south. The 1804 lighthouse did not, as some mistakenly believe, replace the Old Point Comfort Light. Both lights are named after the separate Virginia headlands on which they stand guard, and these were likely given their names long ago by early Tidewater settlers.

In 1801 Congress appropriated $5,000—a handsome sum at the time—to establish a light station on New Point Comfort, at the entrance to Mobjack Bay. Government officials considered the expenditure justified, because the light would be of particular, strategic importance for shipping. Vessels steering to the west of the light would enter the York River, while those steering to the east and north were bound for the upper Chesapeake. The project took three years to complete, and the light entered service late in 1804. Elzie Burroughs, the station's first keeper, received his appointment from President Thomas Jefferson.

In 1852 the newly appointed Lighthouse Board sent inspection teams to examine thoroughly all of the nation's navigational aids. At New Point Comfort, the inspectors found the half-century-old tower still in excellent condition. They reported that keeper Isaac Foster, a retired sea captain, maintained his light with the assistance of a female slave. The inspectors apparently saw nothing exceptional in this arrangement, but they did note that Foster received no allowance beyond his salary of $400 per year for the employment of his "assistant."

During the Civil War a Confederate raiding party attacked the lighthouse and knocked it out of operation. It was not repaired and relit until after the war ended in 1865.

Congress got very good value for its money. The sixty-three-foot, octagonal sandstone tower still stands, virtually unchanged, after nearly two centuries. Unfortunately, the station no longer serves navigators except as a daymark. Automated in 1919, it was finally decommissioned and abandoned during the 1950s. In 1981 Virginia's Mathews County restored the lighthouse as a memorial to local mariners who have lost their lives at sea.

## HOW TO GET THERE:

*Located on a small island surrounded by shallows and mudflats, the New Point Comfort Lighthouse can be reached only by boat.*

Built on an open-water caisson, this lighthouse warns ships away from the "Middle Ground," an L-shaped shoal threatening traffic in the heart of the Newport News Harbor (Hampton Roads), one of the nation's busiest. Its white light flashing every six seconds, the Newport News Middle Ground Light remains in operation today, more than a century after it was completed in 1891. It is easy to see why caisson lighthouses of this type are sometimes called "spark plugs." (© Mark Riddick/New Light Photography)

# OLD POINT COMFORT LIGHT

*Fort Monroe, Virginia – 1802*

Among the earliest lighthouses constructed in the Chesapeake Bay itself was a stubby, fifty-four-foot tower built in 1802 at Fort Monroe. The light marked the mouth of the James River and the entrance to Hampton Roads.

Because of its strategic location, the lighthouse saw plenty of conflicts; several crucial battles were fought within sight of the keepers in the lantern. During the War of 1812, British troops under Admiral Cockburn successfully stormed Fort Monroe and later used the lighthouse as a watchtower. Half a century later, the ironclad *Virginia* steamed past the Point Comfort Light on its way to do battle with the *Monitor*. Following the Civil War, Confederate president Jefferson Davis was imprisoned in a Fort Monroe cell not far from the tower.

Fort Monroe remains an active military post and is home of the Army Training Command. The lighthouse stands in the middle of Officers' Row.

## HOW TO GET THERE:

To reach the fort drive west from Norfolk on I–64; then take the first exit after you emerge from the tunnel under Hampton Roads. The sentry at the Fort Monroe gate can provide directions to the lighthouse.

The tower is not open to the public, but visitors are more than welcome at the Casement Museum, located a short distance from the lighthouse. A self-guided tour starting at the museum leads visitors through the historic fort.

Entrance to the fort and museum are free, and both are open daily. For more information contact the Casement Museum, P.O. Box 341, Fort Monroe, VA 23651; (804) 727–3391.

*British troops used the Fort Monroe lighthouse as a watchtower during the War of 1812.*

# LIGHTSHIP *PORTSMOUTH*

*Portsmouth, Virginia – 1916*

The job of a lighthouse is to guide ships. Ironically, some lighthouses are actually ships themselves. Equipped with lanterns and lenses, these lightships are anchored over remote shoals where lighthouses would be too dangerous or too expensive to build.

In 1915 fifty-five lightships were stationed in U.S. waters. But lighthouse builders have since found ways to replace many lightships with permanent offshore structures, and improvements in navigational aids have made others unnecessary. All but a handful of the old lightships are now gone, and no lightship stations remain.

The vessel now called the *Portsmouth* was commissioned in 1916. Known to lighthouse officials as *LV 101*, it served more than forty-eight years at posts off the coasts of Virginia, Delaware, and Maryland. Retired from active service in 1964, the ship was moved to dry land beside the busy waterfront at Portsmouth, Virginia.

### HOW TO GET THERE:

The lightship, located beside the busy Portsmouth waterfront, is open Tuesday through Saturday from 10:00 A.M. to 5:00 P.M. and Sunday from 1:00 to 5:00 P.M. The $1.50 pass is good for the Naval Shipyard, the Art Center, the Children's Museum, and the Lightship Museum. For more information, contact the Portsmouth Lightship Museum, London Slip, Portsmouth, VA 23704; (804) 393–8741.

*The lightship* Portsmouth *guided ships off the coasts of Virginia, Delaware, and Maryland. The crew's quarters, the galley, and the engine room look as if the crew is just on leave and could return at any moment to take the ship to sea. The beds are made, and the galley appears well stocked for the next meal. Photos and artifacts tell the story of life on a lightship during the early twentieth century.*

# LIGHTHOUSES OF CAPE HENRY

*Virginia Beach, Virginia – 1792 and 1881*

People talked about placing a lighthouse on Cape Henry, at the entrance to the Chesapeake Bay, a long time before anyone actually got around to building one. Among the numerous projects undertaken by Virginia's flamboyant Alexander Spotswood, who governed the colony for the British during the early 1700s, was the construction of a light tower at the mouth of the Chesapeake. Every inch the cavalier, the governor was given to flights of romantic fancy; his ambitious proposals usually generated a great many toasts and a lot of high-toned conversation, but not much action. For instance, in 1716 Spotswood decided to explore the unpopulated wilderness west of the Virginia tidewater, and he actually set off into the backcountry wearing a green-velvet riding suit and sporting a sweeping plume in his hat. Spotswood apparently saw his journey into the wilds as something of

an extended foxhunt, since he took with him a dozen properly attired Virginia gentlemen and a wagon creaking under a heavy load of wine and liquor. A few days after they had departed, Spotswood and his companions returned to their plantations in much too tipsy a condition to remember anything they had seen.

Spotswood could not interest the British government in his lighthouse idea, but the governor's proposal attracted numerous advocates in Virginia's House of Burgesses as well as among prominent planters and merchants throughout the Chesapeake region. Like the governor himself, however, they all found it far easier to raise a glass of port than to finance and construct a tall stone tower. Nearly half a century after Spotswood and his plumed hat had passed from the scene, the Cape Henry tower still had not been built.

*One of the oldest lighthouse towers in America, the Old Cape Henry Light was built in 1789. The cape, one of two enclosing the Chesapeake Bay, was named for one of the sons of King James I of England.*

In 1774 the colonies of Maryland and Virginia finally decided to move ahead with the project. Tons of stone were piled up at the construction site, but funding ran out while the foundation was being laid. Before more money could be found, the drums of the Revolutionary War put a stop to the effort. After the war stonemasons understandably balked at working for worthless Continental dollars. So it was not until 1791, shortly after adoption of the Constitution and the establishment of a stable currency, that the project could continue. The nation's first federal Congress authorized a lighthouse for Cape Henry and appropriated $24,077 for its construction.

Contractor John McComb, hired by Secretary of the Treasury Alexander Hamilton, had at first hoped to use the stone stockpiled for the tower by colonial builders twenty years earlier. Unfortunately, most of the big stones had sunk so deep into the sand that they could not be salvaged. Using freshly quarried sandstone, McComb completed the ninety-foot tower in the fall of 1792.

McComb and his crews built a solid lighthouse; the tower has stood for almost 200 years, through several wars and countless gales. The Confederates put the light out of service briefly at the beginning of the Civil War, but the Lighthouse Board had lamps burning again by 1863.

In 1870 a network of large cracks began to split the tower. Fearing that the lighthouse would crack open and collapse, the board had a cast-iron tower built about 100 yards to the southeast. Standing 156 feet tall, the new tower received a first-order Fresnel lens and began service to the Chesapeake shipping lanes on December 15, 1881. Both towers still stand today.

## HOW TO GET THERE:

Both of these lighthouses are located on the grounds of Fort Story at the north end of Virginia Beach. To reach the fort, take U.S. Highway 60 south from Norfolk. The entrance to the fort, an active military post, is about 10 miles from downtown Norfolk. The guard at the gate will provide a car pass and directions to the lighthouse.

A National Historic Landmark, the old 1791 lighthouse is open for visitors to climb the 90-foot tower every day of the week from March 15 through October 31 from 10:00 A.M. to 5:00 P.M. Children must be at least 7 years old and be accompanied by an adult. A small admission fee is charged except for military personnel.

For more information call the Cape Henry Light at (804) 422–9421.

*Lighthouse towers stand watch at Fort Story.*

# BIBLIOGRAPHY

Adams, William Henry Davenport. *Lighthouses and Lightships: A Descriptive and Historical Account of Their Mode of Construction and Organization.* New York: Scribner, 1870.

Adamson, Hans Christian. *Keepers of the Light.* New York: Greenberg, 1955.

Beaver, Patrick. *A History of Lighthouses.* Secaucus, N.J.: Citadel, 1972.

de Gast, Robert. *The Lighthouses of the Chesapeake.* Baltimore: Johns Hopkins University, 1973.

Hamilton, Harlan. *Lights and Legends: A Historical Guide to Lighthouses of Long Island Sound, Fishers Island Sound and Block Island Sound.* Stamford, Ct.: Wescott Cove Publishing Co., 1987.

Holland, Francis Ross, Jr. *America's Lighthouses: Their Illustrated History Since 1716.* Brattleboro, Vt.: Stephen Greene Press, 1972.

Moe, Christine. *Lighthouses and Lightships.* Monticello, Ill.: Moe, 1979.

Pouliot, Richard and Julie Pouliot. *Shipwrecks on the Virginia Coast.* Centreville, Md.: Tidewater, 1986.

Putnam, George R. *Sentinel of the Coasts.* New York: Norton, 1937.

Rattray, Jeannette Edwards. *Perils of the Port of New York: Maritime Disaster from Sandy Hook to Execution Rocks.* New York: Dodd, Mead, 1973.

Scheina, Robert L. "The Evolution of the Lighthouse Tower." In *Lighthouses: Then and Now* (supplement to the U.S. Coast Guard Commandant's Bulletin).

Shomette, Donald. *Shipwrecks on the Chesapeake.* Centreville, Md.: Tidewater, 1982.

Snow, Edward Rowe. *Famous Lighthouses of America.* New York: Dodd, Mead, 1955.

_____. *Famous New England Lighthouses.* Boston: Yankee Publishing, 1945.

United States Coast Guard. *Historically Famous Lighthouses.* CG-232, 1986.

_____. *Chronology of Aids to Navigation and the Old Lighthouse Service.* CG-485, 1974.

Weiss, George. *The Lighthouse Service: Its History, Activity and Organization.* Baltimore: Johns Hopkins University, 1926.

# LIGHTHOUSES INDEX

*Numerals in italics indicate photograph/legend only.*

# FOR FURTHER INFORMATION
## ON LIGHTHOUSES

**Lighthouse Preservation Society**
P.O. Box 736
Rockport, MA 01966

LPS is known as an advocacy group and sponsors lighthouse conferences.

**Lighthouse Digest**
P.O. Box 1690
Wells, ME 04090
(207) 646–0515

The *Digest* publishes an interesting monthly devoted to lighthouse news.

**Lighthouses of the Virginia Sea**
c/o Christine Koch
Route 2, Box 2
Louisa, VA 23093

Organization publishes a quarterly newsletter about Virginia lighthouses.

**U.S. Lighthouse Society**
244 Kearny Street, 5th Floor
San Francisco, CA 94108
(415) 362–7255

Members receive an interesting quarterly magazine about lighthouses, and the society conducts
    worldwide tours of lighthouses.

**Outer Banks Lighthouse Society**
301 Driftwood Street
Nags Head, NC 27959
(919) 441–4232

Organization publishes an in-depth, quarterly newsletter about local lighthouses with emphasis
    on the keepers and their families.

**U.S. Coast Guard**
Historian's Office G-CP/H
2100 2nd Street, SW
Washington, DC 20593

The Coast Guard History Office maintains operational records and historical materials related to
    the U.S. Coast Guard and its predecessor agencies.

**National Archives**
Record Group 26
Washington, DC 20480

Record Group 26 constitutes records of the Bureau of Lighthouses and its predecessors, 1789–1939,
    as well as U.S. Coast Guard records, 1828–1947, and cartographic and audiovisual materials,

1855–1963. These records are at the main archives building in Washington, D.C. Some records, such as the individual lighthouse logs, are stored at the Suitland, Maryland, branch.

**U.S. Coast Guard, 5th District**
431 Crawford Street
Portsmouth, VA 23704

The Fifth Coast Guard District is responsible for the operation and maintenance of the light-houses along the mid-Atlantic coast. For permission to visit lighthouses not generally open to the public, contact the public affairs officer at this address.

*For information about the Cape May Light, contact:*

**Mid-Atlantic Center for Arts**
P.O. Box 340
Cape May, NJ 08204

**Chesapeake Chapter of the USLS:**
c/o Herb Entwistle
211 Ross Drive, SW
Vienna, VA 22180
(703) 281–9040

Chapter conducts trips to the Chesapeake Bay lighthouses.

**National Park Service**
Maritime Initiative
P.O. Box 37127
Washington, DC 20013-7127
(202) 343–9508

The Maritime Initiative is a database that contains the most accurate information available about American lighthouses.

*For information about the Sandy Hook Light, contact:*

**National Park Service**
Gateway National Recreation Area
Sandy Hook Unit
P.O. Box 530
Fort Hancock, NJ 07732

*For information about the Fire Island Light, contact:*

**National Park Service**
Fire Island National Seashore
120 Laurel Street
Patchogue, NY 11772

*For information about the Montauk Light, contact:*

**Montauk Historical Society**
RFD 2, Box 112
Montauk, NY 11954

# PHOTO INFORMATION

The photographs taken in this book were taken on Fuji chrome color film and T-MAX black-and-white film. Other films, I'm sure, would have worked just as well; but being a travel photographer who takes trips constantly, I've learned to simplify what I take in my travel bag. The typical contents include two Nikon 8008 camera bodies with a small assortment of lenses: a 24-mm wide angle, a 35-135-mm zoom, a short telephoto lens such as an f2 85 mm, and a longer 70-300-mm zoom. Then there's my tripod; yes, *tripod*. When I was a young newspaper photographer, I thought tripods were for novice photographers who were afraid to blur images. Now I think only the overconfident do *not* use them. And for lighthouses, a tripod is a necessity unless you want only full-daylight pictures. In addition, there are in my camera case two little pieces of glass that I'm always looking for, and one or the other will be on my camera lens most of the time when I am shooting. One is a polarizing filter that enhances the color in bright, sunlit shots; the other is a warming filter that prevents the bluish cast that occurs on cloudy days and in deep shade on sunny days.

The photograph of Hooper Strait Light on page 64 exemplifies the effect of a polarizing filter. The deep blue sky and rich color have been enhanced by the filter. It is easy to use; place it on the lens and rotate it until it looks best. The camera meter automatically adjusts the exposure.

There are two light shows, sunrise and dusk, at every lighthouse each day; these are the coveted times I like to be shooting. At most working lighthouses the light comes on half an hour before sunset and stays on for half an hour after sunrise, giving photographers an opportunity to work with a beacon's light shining. See the Old Point Comfort photo on page 77 for an example.

When photographing lighthouses, look for details such as stairways. Doorways, cornerstone dates, and windows all make good detail shots. At lighthouses where you can tour inside, objects and artifacts add interest, as exemplified in the photo on page 5.

A lighthouse's beam of light will look brighter if you can get a high elevation with your camera. Remember, the Fresnel lens is concentrating the light into a narrow beam; if you are standing at the base of the light, that beam is far above your head. Back off several hundred feet; the light will look a great deal more intense.

Try walking around the lighthouse, if possible, and viewing it from *all* the compass points. You may like one of the less-photographed points of view better than the usual angle. Remember, there is no "right" and "wrong" way to photograph a lighthouse. It's your film and imagination. Do it any way you like.

—BRUCE ROBERTS

# ABOUT THE AUTHORS

BRUCE ROBERTS and his wife, Cheryl, who helped with the research for this book, live on North Carolina's Outer Banks, not far from the Bodie Island Lighthouse. For many years Bruce was senior travel photographer for *Southern Living* magazine. He started his career working as a photographer for newspapers in Tampa, Florida, and Charlotte, North Carolina. He is the recipient of many photography awards, and some of his photos are in the permanent collection of the Smithsonian Institution. Recently Bruce and Cheryl opened the Lighthouse Gallery & Gifts, a store devoted to lighthouse books, artifacts, and collectibles, in Nags Head.

RAY JONES is a freelance writer and publishing consultant living in Surry, a small town on the coast of Maine. He began his writing career working as a reporter for weekly newspapers in Texas. He has served as an editor for Time-Life Books, as founding editor of *Albuquerque Living* magazine, as a senior editor and writing coach at *Southern Living* magazine, and as publisher of Country Roads Press. Ray grew up in Macon, Georgia, where he was inspired by the writing of Ernest Hemingway and William Faulkner, and worked his way through college as a disc jockey.